Kay with Love Christmas '77

W9-ACB-317

Emmet Fox's
Golden Keys
to
Successful
Living

Emmet Fox's
Golden Keys
to
Successful
Living

&

Reminiscences

Herman Wolhorn

HARPER & ROW, PUBLISHERS
New York, Hagerstown, San Francisco, London

All the books by Emmet Fox from which the extracts in this book have been taken are published by Harper & Row. Titles and dates are as follows:

ALTER YOUR LIFE, 1950
DIAGRAMS FOR LIVING, 1968
FIND AND USE YOUR INNER POWER, 1941
MAKE YOUR LIFE WORTH WHILE, 1946
POWER THROUGH CONSTRUCTIVE THINKING, 1940
THE SERMON ON THE MOUNT, 1938
STAKE YOUR CLAIM, 1952
THE TEN COMMANDMENTS, 1953

EMMET FOX'S GOLDEN KEYS TO SUCCESSFUL LIVING and REMINISCENCES. Copyright ©1977 by Herman Wolhorn. All rights reserved. Printed in the United States of America. No part of this book may be used or reproduced in any manner whatsoever without written permission except in the case of brief quotations embodied in critical articles and reviews. For information address Harper & Row, Publishers, Inc., 10 East 53rd Street, New York, N.Y. 10022. Published simultaneously in Canada by Fitzhenry & Whiteside Limited, Toronto.

FIRST EDITION

Designed by Janice Stern

Library of Congress Cataloging in Publication Data

Wolhorn, Herman.
   Emmet Fox's golden keys to successful living.
   1. Fox, Emmet. 2. New Thought. 3. Clergy—
Biography. I. Title.
BF648.F6W64 1977   248′.4′0924   76–62930
ISBN 0–06–069670–2

77 78 79 80 81 10 9 8 7 6 5 4 3 2 1

CONTENTS

PART TWO

Preface

For many years there has been an insistent demand from the followers of Emmet Fox for a biography that would give a more intimate view of the man than his books provide. In one sense the life of Emmet Fox cannot be separated from the teaching he did in person and through his publications, and yet there was a warm, intimate, personal side, known to few rather than to many. And so I have divided this book into two parts. Part One is a summary of the teaching he gave, annotated (in italic type) with personal observations that I experienced during the twenty years we worked together.

Part Two is an intimate view of the Emmet Fox my wife and I knew in our close association with him. I am sure there are many people around the world who could offer other insights of Emmet Fox as they perceived him, but I have confined this account, with few exceptions, to the three of us: Emmet Fox, Blanche Wolhorn, and myself. It is not a chronological account. I have grouped related ideas and events so as to convey a comprehensive portrait of Emmet Fox in his constant search for Truth and in the ongoing work of his Healing Ministry.

I take this opportunity to express my gratitude to Clayton Carlson of Harper & Row, who encouraged the writing of this project, to Eleanor Jordan and Fred Becker, also of Harper, who provided insights about the Emmet Fox books, and to Dr. Fletcher Harding, a special friend of Emmet Fox, whose moving tribute to Dr. Fox at the time of his departure closes the book.

H.W.

Part One

The
Great Golden
Key

Among the golden keys which Emmet Fox has given to his followers, none is more famous than his essay called "The Golden Key." Millions of copies have been sold in many and varied translations. It has appeared in French, German, Spanish, Portuguese, Greek, Russian, and in the Hindustani dialect that Gandhi spoke; and undoubtedly it has been translated into many other languages and dialects by individuals who have had its efficacy proven in their own lives and have wanted to help friends and relatives.

There have been thousands of letters over the years endorsing the value of "The Golden Key," sometimes even desperate in their appeal for a copy, as the request from a woman who wrote for another because "I washed it in the washing machine in the pocket of my apron and now I have no more Golden Key."

It has been paraphrased by a number of religious leaders who have gotten on to its simple recipe for getting out of trouble: "See God where the trouble seems to be; think about God instead of the difficulty." If one can do that successfully, and hundreds of thou-

sands have done so, the trouble evaporates, the diffi-
culty disappears, and only good remains in its place.
   Sometimes people have asked, "How do I think of
God." Emmet Fox has answered that too. There is a
chapter in Alter Your Life *called "The Seven Main*
Aspects of God," which gives the reader, the student,
the practitioner, simple but concrete instructions for
thinking of God in any kind of problem or situation.
He asks:

Have you ever asked yourself the question: What is God
like? We are told to pray by turning away from the problem and thinking about God; but how are we to think
about God? What is His nature? What is His character?
Where is He? Can we really contact Him, and if so, how?

The first and most fundamental thing to realize is that
God is not just a superior kind of man. Most people would
say, "Of course not," but my experience shows me that
even today the majority of people, in their hearts, do think
of God as just a magnified man, an extraordinarily wise
man, a man of infinite power, but still a man. Now such an
idea is really but a projection of their own personalities,
and it requires very little thought to show that such an
idea cannot be true. In philosophy, such a being is called
an anthropomorphic God (from *anthropos*—man, and
morphe—form—see Webster). And no such finite person
could possibly have created the boundless universe that we
see through our telescopes, or the infinite variety of
minute forms that we contact through the microscope; to
say nothing of the infinite creation of which we are still
altogether unaware.

God is infinite which is in-finite or unlimited. Reflect
upon this every day of your life and a lifetime will not be
long enough to grasp all that it means.

A great practical difficulty in discussing God is the fact that we have no suitable pronoun to employ. We have to use the words "he" and "him." We have no alternative, but these words are very misleading because they inevitably suggest a man or male. To say "she" and "her" would be equally absurd, and the word "it," besides seeming to lack in reverence, suggests an inanimate and unintelligent object. The reader is therefore asked to bear in mind that the use of "He" and "Him" is an unavoidable makeshift, and to correct his or her thought accordingly.

There is no way to find God except by *prayer*, and prayer is thinking about God. The Bible says that God is spirit (John 4:24) and that they that worship Him must worship Him in spirit and in truth. To worship Him in spirit means to get a spiritual understanding of His nature, and we shall now endeavor to do this. We shall not attempt to define God because that would be to limit Him, but we get what is for all practical purposes an excellent working knowledge of God. We shall do this by considering different aspects of His nature, one by one.

Of these there are Seven Main Aspects that are more important than any of the others. These are seven fundamental truths about God, and all the others are built up of combinations of some of these seven. These truths never change. They were the same a billion years ago and they will be the same a billion years hence. So naturally it behooves us to get as clear an understanding and as strong a realization as possible of these Seven Main Aspects. This can be done by thinking about them a good deal, comparing one with another, and identifying them in the experiences of everyday life. This is prayer and very powerful prayer too.

The quickest way to solve a particular problem is to meditate on whichever Aspect is the most appropriate in that particular case. Thinking of any Aspect of God will solve a problem, but if you select the right Aspect you will get your result more quickly and more easily.

The First Main Aspect is Life. God is Life. God is not just living, nor does God *give* life, but God *is* Life. God is *your* life. Life is existence or being.

Realize the Aspect of God as Life for healing sickness, for the "getting older" belief, and for any kind of depression or discouragement. If a person seems to lack ambition treat him for life by realizing the presence of Divine Life in him. Of course, you can heal animals and plants too. Animals usually respond quickly to this treatment, and plants very quickly indeed; but one should not try to keep an old animal alive by treatment after it has reached the normal span for its species.

Joy is one of the highest expressions of God as Life. Actually it is a mixture of Life and Love. The Bible says that "the sons of God shout for joy," and it means that one is radiantly happy because he is expressing the Life of God in him at a high level or potential.

The Second Main Aspect of God is Truth. God is Truth. God is not truthful but Truth itself, and does not change. There are many things which are relatively true at certain times and places only; but God is absolute Truth at all times and in all circumstances.

To know the Truth about any condition heals it. Jesus said, "Know the truth, and the truth shall make you free" (John 8:32). Truth is the great healer.

You should also realize God as Truth when you want information on any subject, or if you suspect that you have to deal with deceit or falsehood. If you have reason to believe that someone is trying to deceive you, think of God as Truth and claim that Divine Truth dwells in the person concerned and is expressed through him. If you realize this clearly enough he will then speak the truth. When you have to transact any important business such as signing a lease or a contract, spend a few minutes realizing Divine Truth and if there is anything you should know it will come out.

Realizing God as Truth will save you hours of work in research in any field. You will be led to the right book or the right place or the right person without loss of time; or the necessary information will come to you in some other way.

The Third Main Aspect of God is Love. God is Love. God is not loving but Love itself, and it would probably be true to say that of all the Seven Main Aspects this is the most important one for us in practice. There is no condition that enough Love will not heal,* and where there is good will it is not difficult to develop a sufficient sense of Love for the purpose of healing.

The best way to rid yourself of fear is to realize Divine Love. If you love God (by affirming it and meaning it) more than you love your problem, your sickness, your grievance, your lack, or your fear, you will be healed. If you could feel a sense of Divine Impersonal Love toward everyone, no one could hurt you.

There is only one remedy for fear, and that is to get some sense of Divine Love, by thinking about it, analyzing it, claiming it, and expressing it in practice.

Do not talk about your prayers. Do not tell people that you are praying for such and such a thing, or in such and such a way. Keep the affairs of your soul secret. When you get a demonstration do not run around and tell everyone about it immediately. Keep it to yourself until it has had

*See chapter on "Love."

time to crystallize. When Jesus healed people, he said, "Go away and tell no one."

The Fourth Main Aspect of God is Intelligence. God is not merely intelligent. God is Intelligence itself. When you clearly realize that this is an intelligent universe it will make a major difference in your life. It is obvious that in an intelligent universe there cannot be any disharmony because all ideas must work together for the common good.

It is especially important to realize that God is Intelligence because it sometimes happens that when people outgrow the childish idea that God is just a magnified man, they go to the opposite extreme and think of God as merely a blind force like gravity or electricity. This means that they have lost all sense of the Love and Fatherhood of God, and such an idea is very little better than a subtle form of atheism. Indeed, this standpoint is not very far removed from the attitude of the materialist who is usually a great believer in what he calls the laws of Nature.

Although God is not a person in the usual sense of the word, *He has every quality of personality except its limitation*. Think of God as a loving Father always ready to heal and comfort. Remember that God knows you and loves you and cares for you—that He is and has infinite Intelligence—that He is and has all Power—that His nature is perfect Divine Love. Turn to God today in the same way and the same spirit as you would have done when you were five or six years of age, but plus the larger understanding that you have since acquired.

When things in your life seem to be going wrong, treat yourself for Intelligence. As a matter of fact you should treat yourself for Intelligence two or three times a week, by thinking about it, and claiming it for yourself. This practice will make every activity of your life more efficient.

The Fifth Main Aspect of God is Soul, spelled with a

capital S. Do not confuse this with soul spelled with a small s, which is what modern psychology calls the psyche, and is another name for your human mind which consists of your intellect and your feelings.*

Soul is the Aspect of God by virtue of which He is able to *individualize* Himself. The word "individual" means *un*divided (see Webster), and God has the power of *individualizing* Himself without, so to speak, breaking Himself into parts.

So your real self, the Christ within, the spiritual man, the I Am, or the divine spark, as it is variously called, is an individualization of God. *You are the presence of God at the point where you are.* This does not, of course, mean that you are an absurd little personal God. You are an individualization of the one and only God (John 10:34).

The Aspect of God as Soul is the one to realize when you are called upon to perform some task or undertake some responsibility that seems too great for you. If you get this clear enough you will be amazed at how well everything will go, and you will have permanently entered a higher category of work. Whatever you have to do, it is good practice to remind yourself that it is God doing it through you. As someone has aptly said, "Man is the by-means-of," the channel through which God works.

The Sixth Main Aspect of God is Spirit. God is Spirit (John 4:24). Spirit is that which cannot be destroyed or damaged or hurt, or degraded or soiled in any way. Spirit cannot deteriorate. It cannot grow old or tired. It cannot know sin, or condemnation, or resentment, or disappointment. It is the opposite of matter. Matter is always deteriorating and wearing out. This is really a splendid thing because it means that the world is constantly being re-

*See "The Four Horsemen" in *Alter Your Life.*

newed. Much of the material progress is due to this fact. For example, if automobiles did not wear out we might still be using the primitive models of forty or fifty years ago. We should never try to hold on mentally to material objects, but be ever ready to renew and improve upon them.

All beauty, all good, all joy, are the Presence of God apprehended through the veil of matter.

The time to realize the Aspect of God as Spirit is when something seems to be damaged or soiled or in decay. If you can realize the presence of Spirit where the trouble seems to be the evil condition will begin to improve, and if your realization is sufficiently clear the condition will be completely healed.

When Jesus saw the man with the withered hand he realized that in Truth that hand was spiritual—and the hand was healed. When you realize that any given thing is not in reality matter, but a spiritual idea seen in a limited way, that "thing" changes for the better. It matters not whether it be a living thing like a part of your body, an animal, or a plant; or whether it is what we call an inanimate object, the law is the same. The so-called inanimate objects are really spiritual ideas—a table, your watch, your shoes, your house—seen in the limited (clouded) way that we call matter. An animal is a wonderful grouping of God's ideas in which Intelligence is a principal component, but it is not an individualization such as man is.

Do not theorize too much about this subject but try a few practical experiments. When something is giving trouble, affirm and try to realize that in reality it is a spiritual idea—and watch what happens. If an automobile, or any other kind of mechanism, is giving trouble, try treating it. I know that this will sound fantastic to people unacquainted with spiritual law, and so I say, do not be obstinate but try it.*

The Seventh Main Aspect of God is Principle, and this is probably the one that is least understood. People do not usually think of God as Principle, but such He is. The simplest example of an ordinary everyday principle is "Water seeks its own level." This is a principle. It is not a particular drop of water nor the course taken by a particular drop of water in a particular locality. It is a general principle that is true of all water everywhere on earth. It is not a particular thing or a particular action. It is a principle.

This principle, and every other principle, was true a billion years ago and it will be true a billion years hence. Principle never changes.

God is the Principle of perfect harmony and God does not change, so perfect harmony is the nature of His creation. Prayer is answered because God is principle, and when we pray rightly we bring ourselves into harmony with the Law of Being. Scientific Prayer does not try to change the Law. It does not try to bring about exceptions in our favor. It does not ask God to change the laws of nature for our temporary convenience, but it tunes us in, so to speak, with Divine Principle; and then we find things coming right, because in that particular situation there is perfect harmony and right action that we have not seen at the moment. So it is always a question of tuning in to God through prayer.

A simple but powerful treatment is to remind yourself— God is Principle, the Principle of perfect harmony, and therefore perfect harmony is the Law of Being in this case.

This Aspect of God, namely, Principle, may be used at

*A wonderful example of treatment of an automobile will be found in the chapter "Along the Road"—The Changing Forties.

any time, but it is especially helpful when you are feeling discouraged about your prayers, and in cases where there seems to be a great deal of ill feeling or prejudice involved. In other cases where there seems to be any sense of vindictiveness or spite, such things will melt away under the realization that Divine Principle is the only Power that exists, and that there simply is no false personality to think evil of that kind.

These are the Seven Main Aspects of God and one cannot really draw a hard and fast line between them. In practice it is often better to handle a particular problem by realizing two or more of them.

There are many attributes of God, such as Wisdom, Beauty, Joy, and so forth, but they are compounds, made up of two or more of the Seven Main Aspects.

There are two synonyms for the word God—Mind and Cause. Each means exactly the same as the word God itself. God is the religious name for the Creator of all things. Mind is the metaphysical name, and Cause is the natural science name for God. Anything that has any real existence is an idea in the One Mind; and this is the metaphysical interpretation of the universe. From the natural science point of view we may say that all creation is the result or effect of One Cause (God) and that there are no secondary causes. A cause cannot be known directly. It can be known only by its effect, and so the universe is the manifestation or effect of Cause or God, and because God is good, it must be good too.

Change
Your Mind

While practicing his profession as electrical engineer in London, Emmet Fox began reading about the American metaphysical movement. He soon found that others were interested in it too, one being a giant among advanced thinkers of that day, Judge Thomas Troward. Dr. Fox worked with Judge Troward who eventually suggested E. F. go out and spread the teaching.

For several years before coming to America Emmet Fox lectured extensively throughout England and Scotland at New Thought Centers, Psychology Clubs, and Higher Thought Centers. The lectures became so popular that he established regular Sunday evening meetings in Wigmore Hall in London.

His central theme at that time was "Alter Your Life," because he felt the idea that would get people out of their narrow outlook and hidebound ways was to change their minds, to alter their reactions to circumstances and conditions. He stressed this so much that among his eager followers he was known as "Alter-Your-Life Fox."

Of course, he brought this "golden key" to America
and it has changed innumerable lives. He begins:

There is no need to be unhappy. There is no need to be sad. There is no need to be disappointed, or oppressed, or aggrieved. There is no need for illness or failure or discouragement. There is no *necessity* for anything but success, good health, prosperity, and an abounding interest and joy in life.

Success and happiness are the natural condition of mankind. It is actually easier for us to demonstrate these things than the reverse. Bad habits of thinking and acting may obscure this fact for a time, just as a wrong way of walking or sitting, or holding a pen or a musical instrument may seem to be easier than the proper way because we have accustomed ourselves to it; but the proper way is the easier nevertheless.

You should never "put up" with anything. You should never be willing to accept less than Health, Harmony, and Happiness. These things are your Divine Right as the sons and daughters of God, and it is only a bad habit, unconscious as a rule, that causes you to be satisfied with less.

You can have prosperity no matter what your present circumstances may be. You can have health and physical fitness. You can have a happy and joyous life. You can have a good home of your own; and congenial friends and comrades. You can have a full, free, joyous life, independent and untrammeled. You can become your own master or your own mistress. But to do this you must definitely seize the rudder of your own destiny and steer boldly and firmly for the port that you intend to make.

Well, what are you doing about your future? Are you content to let things just drift along as they are, hoping, like Mr. Micawber, for something to "turn up"? If you are, be assured that there is no escape in that way. Nothing ever will turn up unless you exercise your Free Will and go out and turn it up for yourself by becoming acquainted with the Laws of Life and applying them to your own individual conditions. That is the only way. Otherwise the years will pass all too swiftly, leaving you just where you are now, if not worse off, for there is no limit to the result of thought either for good or for evil.

Man has dominion over all things when he knows the Law of Being, and obeys it. The Law gives you independence so that you can build your own life in your own way. The Law gives you power to attain prosperity and position without infringing the rights and opportunities of anyone else. The Law gives you power to overcome your own weaknesses and faults of character. The Law will endow you with the gift of what is called Originality—the doing of things in a new way which is a better way, and different from anyone else's way. The Law will give you authority over the past as well as the future and make you master of Karma instead of its slave.

Oh, how I love Thy Law.

Do not "put off" your study of the Law any longer. Procrastination, we are told, is the thief of time; and another proverb says still more emphatically that Hell itself is paved, not with evil intentions, but with good ones. It is of the postponer that the Law says, *Thou shalt hear the Never Never whispered by the phantom years*, but the path of the Wise (the righteous or Right Thinker) shineth more and more unto the Perfect Day.

So it is important to know what the Law of Being is. The Bible handles it in various ways. In the Old Testament it says, "As a man thinketh in his heart [subconscious] so is he." In the New Testament it says, "Whatsoever a man soweth, that shall he also reap." In metaphysics we often say, "Thoughts are things," or "As within, so without."

Emmet Fox in his "The Ten Commandments" gives a very concise and modern definition. He says:

There is one great fundamental law, the Law of Being, the summing up of all laws in life. It is this: whatever comes to you, whatever happens to you, whatever surrounds you, will be in accordance with your consciousness, and nothing else; that whatever is in your consciousness must happen, no matter who tries to stop it; and whatever is not in your consciousness cannot happen.

So as we study this Law of Being, as we contemplate the full import of it, we more and more become masters of our own destiny.

Take stock of your life this very day. Sit down quietly by yourself with a pencil and paper, and write down the three things that you most wish for in life. Be quite frank about this. Write down the things you *really* wish for, not things that you think you *ought* to wish for. Be specific, not vague. Then write down underneath three things or conditions that you wish to *remove* from your life. Again, be definite and specific.

If you do this candidly you now have an extremely valuable analysis of your own mentality. In course of time this will tell you a great many things about yourself which you do not at present suspect, things far beyond the range of the actual six points themselves, and as your knowledge of spiritual Truth increases, you will be able to handle the new knowledge about yourself in a surprising way.

Now having got your six points in front of you, work on each one separately for a few minutes with all the spiritual and metaphysical knowledge that you possess. In the beginning do not be concerned if you feel your spiritual knowledge is meager. Your knowledge will increase by leaps and bounds as you repeat your treatment each day for a month. Do not miss a single day, and by the end of that time it will be very unusual if a really striking change for the better has not manifested itself in your conditions.

For those unfamiliar with spiritual treatment, a simple but quite effective method of working is this: Claim gently but definitely that the Great Creative Life Force of the Universe is bringing each of the first three things into your life in Its own way, in Its own time, and in Its own form. Then claim that the same Great Power is dissolving each of the latter three, also in Its own way. Do not try to dictate the exact form in which the new conditions shall come about. Do not be tense or vehement. *Do not let anyone else know that you are doing this.* Do not look impatiently every day for results, but make your treatment, and forget it until next day. *And in quietness and confidence shall be your strength.*

> *Having laid down the rules for a more abundant and successful life and realizing that so many people have a great fear of change, Emmet Fox emphasizes that Life is Change, and gives comfort to the doubtful: "I see the Angel of God in every change."*

This is an affirmation that you should write inside the cover of your pocketbook and also in some prominent place at home where you will often see it. It is one of the keys of a harmonious and progressive life. Especially in these critical times, it will stand out in your life like a lighthouse in a stormy sea. Change is the law of growth; and growth is the law of life. Without change there can be no growth, and without continual growth, life fades out of any form, leaving what we call death.

There is no greater mistake than to be afraid of change,

and yet many intelligent people dread it and cling to what is customary and familiar. To be afraid of change is to doubt the providence of God. It is an unintelligent fear of the unknown. If it were not for the blessing of change, men would still be primitive savages living in caves, and you yourself would still be a child mentally and physically, would you not?

Welcome every change that comes into any phase of your life; insist that it is going to turn out for the better—and it will. *See the Angel of God in it*, and that Angel will make all things new.

> *And Emmet Fox gives this final clincher: Change your mind—and keep it changed.*

If some condition in your life is not to your liking, *change your mind about it—and keep it changed.* If someone is displeasing to you, change your mind about him—and keep it changed. If there is some sad memory that haunts you, change your mind about it—and keep it changed.

Most students of metaphysics are ready to change their minds about a problem, especially when they have just been to a lecture or talked with a teacher; but they *do not keep them changed.*

This is the crux of the matter. If you will change your mind concerning anything and *absolutely keep it changed,* that thing must and will change too. It is the keeping up of the change in thought that is difficult. It calls for vigilance and determination. But surely it is worth while, since it is the key to Dominion.

Make an experiment now. Change your mind concerning some particular thing in your life and *keep it changed;*

and I guarantee that you will be amazed and delighted at
the result.

*And then in a spiritual outburst Emmet Fox cites
Jesus as the authority for a complete spiritual change
in this spark of Truth, "You Must be Born Again":*

We are told concerning the teaching of Jesus that the
common people heard him gladly. This could easily have
been inferred from the most superficial study of the Gos-
pels. The "man in the street," unsophisticated by theology
or philosophy, has an intuitive perception of fundamental
Truth when he meets it, that is often lacking in highly
trained minds. Intellectual attainments may easily beget
spiritual pride, and this is the only sin upon which our
Lord was severe. Yet among the learned, too, there were
those, the more spiritually minded, who felt themselves
attracted to the new Teacher. He was unconventional,
hopelessly out of favor with the ecclesiastical authorities, a
flouter of hallowed traditions; and yet, deep calleth unto
deep, and so he had his friends and followers in high places
also.

One of these who felt irresistibly drawn to seek for
further light was Nicodemus. He had the thirst for Divine
things that will not be denied, but moral courage was not
his strong point, and so he sought out the Teacher by
night. That he should have gone at all was proof of the
compelling power of the urge. Clearly the unfoldment of
his spiritual nature was, in spite of defects in character,
the principal thing in his life, and clearly he was dissatisfied with the progress he was making. Jesus, he believed,
had something to give that was vital, and that gift might be
just the secret that had hitherto eluded him, just the key to
unlock the spiritual treasure house of his soul. Jesus might

be able to show why, as we would say in modern phraseology, he had failed to demonstrate. And the Master's explanation was simple, concise, almost overwhelming in its directness. He said: *"You must be born again."*

This statement sums up the whole science of demonstration as it is practiced on the spiritual basis. It is verily a textbook on metaphysics compressed into five words. You stand where you do today, wherever that is, because you are the person that you are. There is only one way under heaven by which you can be brought to stand anywhere else, and that is by becoming another person. The person you are cannot stand anywhere else; a different person cannot stand where you are now. If you wish to go up higher you can do so, and there is no limit to the height which you can attain upon that flight; but *you must be born again!*

Why is it that we make so little progress, compared, that is to say, with what we might and should make in view of the knowledge that we all, in this teaching, possess—at least in theory? Why do we not change day by day and week by week from glory to glory, until our friends can scarcely recognize us for the same men and women? Why should we not march about the world looking like gods, and feeling it; healing instantaneously all who come to us; reforming the sinner; setting the captives free; and generally "doing the works"? "Who did hinder you?"

And the reply is that demonstration, like all other things, has its price; that the price is that we be *born again,* and that in our secret hearts, too often, that is a price that we are not prepared to pay. We are in love with the present man, and all the things that constitute him, and we are not prepared to slay him that the other may be born.

We come into Truth with our little finger, and the great

things will not come to us until we come in with the entire body; and there's the rub.

To come into Truth with your whole body is to bring every conscious thought and belief to the touchstone of Divine Intelligence and Divine Love. It is to reject every single thing, mental or physical, that does not square with that standard. It is to revise every opinion, every habit of thought, every policy, every branch of practical conduct, without any exception whatever.

This, of course, is something absolutely tremendous. It is no mere spring cleaning of the soul. It is nothing less than a wholesale tearing down and rebuilding of the entire house.

It means, as Paul said, "dying daily." It means parting with all the prejudices that you have inherited and acquired during all your life long. It means taking the knife to all the little faults of character, petty vanities, minor deceits, and all those lesser forms of selfishness and pride that crystallize your spiritual joints, and are so dear to you. It may mean giving up the biggest thing in your present life, but if it does—well, that is the price that must be paid.

If you are not prepared to pay this price, well and good; but you must not expect to receive from the Law more than you pay for. A little finger in Truth is well, but it can only produce a little finger result. For a full-length demonstration the whole body must be full of light. *You must be born again.*

A tremendous step in this direction is to put yourself on the Seven Day Mental Diet.* The most important of all factors in your life is the mental diet on which you live. It is the food which you furnish to your mind that deter-

* See *Power Through Constructive Thinking.*

mines the whole character of your life. It is the thoughts
you allow yourself to think, the subjects that you allow
your mind to dwell upon, which make you and your surroundings what they are.

In other words, you choose your life, that is to say, you
choose all the conditions of your life when you choose the
thoughts upon which you allow your mind to dwell.
Thought is the real causative force in life, and there is no
other. You cannot have one kind of mind and another
kind of environment. This means you cannot change your
environment while leaving your mind unchanged. We are
transformed by the renewing of our minds (Rom. 12:2).
So now you will see that your mental diet is really the most
important thing in your whole life.

You must train yourself to choose the subject of your
thinking at any given time, and also to choose the emotional tone, or what we call the mood that colors it. Yes,
you can choose your moods. Indeed if you could not you
would have no real control over your life at all. Moods,
habitually entertained, produce the characteristic disposition of the person concerned, and it is this disposition that
finally makes or mars a person's happiness. Unless you are
determined to cultivate a good disposition, you may as well
give up all hope of getting anything worth while out of
life, and it is kinder to tell you very plainly that this is the
case.

In short, if you want to make your life happy and worth
while you must begin immediately to train yourself in the
habit of thought selection and thought control; and the
foundation of it can be laid within a few days. The way to
do it is this:

Make up your mind to devote one week solely to the
task of building a new habit of thought, and during that
week let everything else in life be unimportant as com-

pared with that. If you will do so, then that week will be the most significant week in your whole life. It will literally be the turning point for you.

This then is your prescription: For seven days you must not allow yourself to dwell for a single moment on any kind of negative thought. You must watch yourself for a whole week as a cat watches a mouse, and you must not under any pretense allow your mind to dwell on any thought that is not positive, constructive, optimistic, kind. This discipline will be so strenuous that you could not maintain it consciously for much more than a week, but I do not ask you to do so. A week will be enough because by that time the habit of constructive thinking will begin to be established. Some extraordinary changes for the better will have come into your life, encouraging you enormously, and then the future will take care of itself.

Do not start it lightly. Think about it for a day or two before you begin. Then start in, and the grace of God go with you. Once you start you must go right through for the seven days. That is essential. The whole idea is to have seven days of unbroken mental discipline in order to get the mind definitely bent in a new direction once and for all.

If you make a false start, or even if you go on well for two or three days and then for any reason "fall off" the diet, the thing to do is to drop the scheme altogether for several days, and then to start again afresh. There must be no jumping on and off, as it were.

You must be quite clear that what this scheme calls for is that you shall not *entertain*, or *dwell upon* negative things. Note this carefully. It does not matter what thoughts may come to you provided you do not entertain them or dwell upon them. Of course, many negative thoughts will come to you all day long. Some of them will just drift into your mind of their own accord seemingly, and these come to you out of the race mind. Other negative thoughts will be given to you by other people, either in conversation or by their conduct, or you will hear disagreeable news perhaps by letter or telephone, or you will see crimes and disasters announced in the newspaper headings. These things, however, do not matter as long as you do not entertain them. In fact, it is these very things that provide the discipline that is going to transform you during this epoch-making, reawakening week.

The thing to do is, directly the negative thought presents itself—turn it out. Turn away from the newspaper; turn out the thought of the unkind letter, or stupid remark, or what not. When the negative thought floats into your mind, immediately turn it out and think of something beautiful, joyous, constructive. Best of all, think of God as explained in "The Golden Key."

A closing word of caution. Do not tell anyone else that you are on the diet, or that you intend to go on it. Keep this tremendous project strictly to yourself. Remember that your soul should be the Secret Place of the Most High. When you have come through the seven days successfully, and secured your demonstration, allow a reasonable time to elapse to establish the new mentality, and then tell the story to anyone else who you think is likely to be helped by it.

And, finally, remember that nothing said or done by anyone else can possibly throw you off the diet. Only your own reaction to the other person's conduct can do that.

The
Power of
Love

When you apply a certain word to God, it must bear the same essential meaning as it does when you apply it to man—otherwise it has no meaning at all. When you say that God is *Love* or *Intelligence*, or that He is *just*, these words must mean substantially what they mean when applied to human beings—or else they are new and special words which therefore carry no significance whatever.

The love of God must be essentially the same thing that we know as the love of the mother for her child, or the love of the artist for his creation, for example. It must be the same quality as these—purified and increased to infinity, of course—but still the same thing in quality; or the term has simply no meaning.

When we say that God is just, we must mean the same kind of thing that we mean when we say that a certain magistrate, or anyone else in authority, acts with justice—or the word has no meaning at all. The justice of God will include an infinite perspective and be quite flawless but it will be essentially the same thing in its nature.

Many people say that God is *Love* and at the same time maintain that He visits finite sin with eternal punishment.

They claim that God is *just*, and yet maintain that people living today are suffering disabilities for a sin supposed to have been committed by Adam thousands of years before they were born. There is still a small number of people who believe that every human being was predestined to heaven or hell before he was created, and that his conduct, good or bad while on this earth, would make no difference to his fate. And the same people say that God is *just*. Obviously in such cases these terms can have no meaning.

If the attributes of God are supposed to signify something different from that conveyed by the ordinary meaning of the words, we cannot know what such meaning is. You might as well say, "God is x + y, but I do not know what these symbols stand for."

The truth is that God *is* Love and Intelligence; and that He works with perfect wisdom and perfect justice to all, at all times, in the ordinary and correct meaning of these words.

"God is light, and in Him is no darkness at all" (I John 1:5).

The ancient Greeks did not have one word for love. They had three. I suppose modern Greeks do too, but Plato and Socrates and others of the Golden Age of Greece were men far ahead of their time, thousands of years ahead in their ideas and expressions. Well, they had three words for love: eros, *erotic or sexual love;* philio, *brotherly love, from which we get the name Philadelphia in the Bible and elsewhere; and* agapē, *spiritual love.*

The Bible recognizes all three, but dwells particularly on brotherly love and urges man to understand and express spiritual love.

Emmet Fox too, in another of his golden keys,

begins "The Golden Gate" with "God is love, and he that dwelleth in love dwelleth in God and God in him" (I John 4:16). He continues:

Love is by far the most important thing of all. It is the Golden Gate of Paradise. Pray for the understanding of love, and meditate upon it daily. It casts out fear. It is the fulfilling of the Law. It covers a multitude of sins. Love is absolutely invincible.

There is no difficulty that enough love will not conquer; no disease that enough love will not heal; no door that enough love will not open; no gulf that enough love will not bridge; no wall that enough love will not throw down; no sin that enough love will not redeem.

It makes no difference how deeply seated may be the trouble, how hopeless the outlook, how muddled the tangle, how great the mistake; a sufficient realization of love will dissolve it all. If only you could love enough you would be the happiest and most powerful being in the world.

Emmet Fox felt so strongly about this message that he had it printed on a large card suitable for wall hanging where one could see it every day. He continues his theme on love:

Statements like Divine Love Never Fails or Divine Love Solves Every Problem are often made by teachers and appear in metaphysical books and magazines—and they are perfectly true. Quite often, however, even people who say they believe them do not prove them in demonstration.

I think the explanation is that, consciously or unconsciously, they think of Divine Love as some sort of Power outside themselves; probably up in the sky like the orthodox heaven; and they expect that presently, if they beg hard enough, this Power will come down and rescue them. As a rule they would not admit harboring such an idea, but I believe that some such idea is what they are actually entertaining.

There is, in fact, no such outside power, and therefore you cannot receive help in that way.

The only place where Divine Love can exist, as far as you are concerned, is in your own heart. Any love that is not *in your heart* does not exist for you, and therefore cannot of course help you in any way.

The thing for you to do, then, is to fill your own heart with Divine Love, by thinking it, feeling it, and expressing it; and when this sense of Divine Love is vivid enough it will heal you and solve your problems, and it will enable you to heal others too. That is the Law of Being and none of us can change it. Now we see why criticism, grumbling, the nursing of grievances, the desire to overreach others, etc., are fatal to demonstration, because they prevent Divine Love from healing us.

And then Emmet Fox gives a treatment for Divine Love, one which he used at many of his public lectures, and which has been used by thousands of people around the world.

My soul is filled with Divine Love. I am surrounded by Divine Love. I radiate Love and Peace to the whole world. I have conscious Divine Love. God is Love, and there is nothing in existence but God and His Self-expression. All men are expressions of Divine Love; therefore, I can meet with nothing but the expressions of Divine Love. Nothing ever takes place but the Self-expressing of Divine Love.

All this is true now. This is the actual case, the actual

state of affairs. I do not have to try to bring this about, but I observe it already in being now. Divine Love is the actual nature of Being. There is only Divine Love, and I know this.

I perfectly understand what Divine Love is. I have conscious realization of Divine Love. The Love of God burns in me for all humanity. I am a lamp of God, radiating Divine Love to all whom I meet, to all whom I think of.

I forgive everything that can possibly need forgiveness—positively everything. Divine Love fills my heart, and all is well. I now radiate Love to the whole universe, excluding no one. I experience Divine Love. I demonstrate Divine Love.

I thank God for this.

Using this treatment as a daily spiritual exercise has helped thousands of people to find the peace and happiness for which they were searching. The idea is not to try to do something with it but to let the treatment work in your consciousness. You might then be tempted to try the "Yoga of Love." Emmet Fox says:

All the old traditions tell us that there is more than one path to the Great Goal. Just as there is more than one road up every great mountain, and yet all roads meet at the top, so in the Spiritual Quest there are several roads, all of which lead in due season to the One Great End.

There is the path of Knowledge. True knowledge of Divine things is one of the appointed paths to attainment; but that path is by no means for everyone. And there is the pathway of Action—of organized activity, perhaps one had better say—and the world needs this too; but this again usually calls for a special gift and special circumstances in which to apply it. And there are others.

The shortest and easiest pathway of all is the Pathway of Love. This really is the Royal Road to the attainment of the Great Goal. It is the simplest of all the paths, and it is the most direct and the easiest too. And it is the one pathway which is open to all, everywhere, irrespective of what their personal conditions or surrounding circumstances may be. For Everyman, everywhere, the true Initiation, through the Yoga of Love, awaits every day.

In metaphysics we understand that Divine Love is the complete expression of all that is meant by the word Religion; that having that we have all, and lacking that, we have nothing. It therefore behooves us to give some little attention to the consideration of what we really mean when we talk about Love.

Of course, it goes without saying that we do not mean personal love. That is well in its own time and place, but it is not what we are considering here. In the Christian teaching, Love stands for something much bigger and finer and more powerful than any merely personal sentiment. Unfortunately, as with many other spiritual ideas, there is no word in the language which is perfectly appropriate to express it. Material language is made to fit material needs, and it simply will not satisfactorily express true spiritual ideas. For these we need the new Tongue of which Jesus spoke. We seldom realize, I think, how much we really are in the hands of the dictionary. We think certain thoughts; we have certain experiences; and then language, with its hard-and-fast boundaries, says, "You shall not say that wonderful thing—you shall say only this"—and we find on paper the pale lifeless shadow of the thing that came to life in our soul.

So there is really no word in modern English to express the true Christian idea of Love. Perhaps we can best approach the idea by saying that Christianity understands by Love the idea of universal good will, but plus something very much more than ordinary good will—that something which is nothing less than God, Himself—Divine Love.

Love is the motive power in Mind, and it is the quality of Love in Mind that leads it to seek for fuller and fuller expression, for Love always must be expressed. What we call Service, to use the term that has happily come into very general use of late, is really Love in Action.

The principal aspects of God are: Life, Truth, and Love. These are the great Trinity in which Mind expresses Itself, and we shall see now in what sense they are one and the same thing. Life is existence, and this is the Truth of Being. Naturally Life must have free expression, and Love is just this very thing, this perfect expression of Life. In other words, what we call Love is really the full and unrestricted expression of Divine Life itself. That is why it always means perfect peace, perfect holiness, perfect beauty, perfect joy—and why Jesus said, "I am come that they might have Life, and that they might have it more abundantly."

Now we see why the converse of Love is fear; and why fear is the supreme enemy of mankind. Everybody recognizes this fact today. All academic psychology is turning its attention to the overcoming of fear, and most schools of philosophy too now teach that fear is the thing that has to be rooted out. And fear turns out to be simply the absence of Love. "Fear hath torment but perfect Love casteth out fear" (I John 4:18).

The only reason we have any fear at all is because we do not love God enough. A great mystic said, "Love God—and do what you please," knowing that with the love of God in our hearts our expression could only be perfect; and a modern seer has told us, "You can get rid of any difficulty whatever from your life as soon as you can love God more than you love the error."

Anger, spite, resentment, and hate—all such things—are

just so many alternative expressions of fear. Jealousy, malice, and "all uncharitableness" denote a belief that there is not enough good to go around and, therefore, if the other fellow gets all that he wants of good, we shall have to go short; and what is this but to constrict the expression of Life in one's own soul?

Now, the absence of Love has exactly this effect upon the soul. Condemnation, resentment, ill will, are just so many constrictions upon the free flow of Life, and since they are allowed to exist, more or less, in so many human souls, is it any wonder that the world is filled with sin, sickness, and death?—that men and women grow old, and tired, and wrinkled, and worn, and ultimately lose their bodies altogether?—that the earth is desolated by wars, and famine, and pestilence?

Thus we begin to see the reason why the Jesus Christ teaching, under whatever name it may have been given out, has always laid so much stress upon the outstanding importance of Love. Unless we build up within our own souls a real and practical Love-consciousness, our other activities will be more or less futile. If we have the impersonal Love-consciousness sufficiently well developed toward all, everything else will follow.

The Pathway of Love which is open to everyone in all circumstances, and upon which you may step at any moment—at this moment if you like—requires no formal introduction, has no entrance examination. It calls for no expensive laboratory in which to work, because your own daily life and your ordinary daily surroundings are your laboratory.

All it does need is that you should begin steadfastly to expel from your mentality every thought of personal condemnation (you must condemn a wrong action, but not the actor), of resentment for old injuries, and of everything which is contrary to the law of Love. You must not allow yourself to hate—either person, or group, or nation, or anything whatever.

You must build up by faithful daily exercise the true Love-consciousness, and then all the rest of spiritual development will follow upon that. Love will heal you. Love will comfort you. Love will guide you. Love will illumine you. Love will redeem you from sin, sickness, and death, and lead you into the promised land, the place that is altogether lovely.

This is the Yoga of Love, and while it requires no equipment beyond the readiness to practice it, yet that readiness is likely to cost so much in the way of effective self-sacrifice that those who truly seek it are comparatively few.

To practice effectively the Yoga of Love is the quickest way to demonstrate over all your own difficulties, and because your mind is part of the race mind, it is actually the quickest and most far-reaching way in which you can elevate the race too.

It is the one path that is in practice open for everyone to enter, at any moment. The plain man earning a modest living in the factory or store can practice the Yoga of Love right there among the very surroundings in which he finds himself. The housekeeper at home, the sailor on the high seas, the farmer in his field, the nurse or the doctor in the ward, have all around them in their duties the perfect material for the Yoga of Love. The only question is whether one is really willing to pay the price—is really prepared to put God first.

As a postscript to this, Emmet Fox emphasized that Divine Love is not something just to be read or prayed about, but it must be in your heart and ex-

pressed in daily life. A beautiful example of this, I believe, is the story of a woman who retired from business, left the city, and took an apartment in a small town. But in her new-found peace and quiet she soon discovered how little there was for her to do. She prayed about the situation for some time, and finally the idea came to her to bake a cake and give it to another person feeling as lonely as she. But to whom? Inquiring of a neighbor, she learned of an elderly woman who was living alone in a big house down the street. She baked her cake, and timidly rang the doorbell. The elderly lady was delighted with her mission and immediately invited her in.

This was the beginning of a friendship that lasted until the elderly lady passed on. The other woman was saddened by her departure, but it was not long before a letter arrived from an attorney. It contained a check for ten thousand dollars with the stipulation that it be spent for a trip around the world. Then the woman remembered that once she had casually mentioned to the elderly lady that she had always wanted to travel.

Love had been at work all the time, for what she had done for the elderly lady was exactly that—a labor of love which had turned into a loving friendship.

Love acts the part.

An Angel
on Your
Shoulder

Emmet Fox not only preached the Truth but he told his students how to use it—"how to do it," as so many have said. It was this practical approach that was instrumental in bringing about change in so many lives around the world. Emmet Fox realized that at rock bottom what everyone wants is to get his or her life in order, to reap the rich harvest which is one's divine birthright. This is quite different from what people sometimes think they are entitled to. Many people have thought that the world owes them a living; but the truth is that one can only claim what is his or hers by right of consciousness.

So here is a collection of Emmet Fox's golden keys linked onto one golden key ring:

There is only one method of spiritual progress, and that is by the Practice of the Presence of God, whether we call this Scientific Prayer or Spiritual Treatment. There is no other way. Mankind is continually seeking to discover a short cut of some kind or other, because the carnal mind is constitutionally lazy; but as usual the lazy man takes the most pains in the long run, and having wasted his time in wandering up bypaths, he is ultimately driven by failure and suffering to the realization of the grand truth that *there is no substitute for prayer.*

The first step that the earnest student must take is to settle on a definite method of working, selecting whichever one seems to suit him best, practicing it conscientiously every day, and sticking to one method long enough to give it a fair chance.

Having got your method, set to work definitely on some concrete problem in your life, choosing preferably whichever is causing you the most trouble at the moment, or, better still, *whatever it is that you are most afraid of.* Work at it steadily and if nothing has happened, if no improvement at all shows itself within, say, a couple of weeks, then try it on another problem. If you still get no result, then scrap that method and adopt a new one. Remember, *there is a way out*; that is as certain as the rising of the sun. The problem really is, not the getting rid of your difficulties, but the finding of your own best method of doing it.

If ill health is your difficulty, do not rest until you have brought about at least one bodily healing. There is no malady that has not been healed by someone at some time, and what others have done you can do, for God is Principle, and Principle changes not.

If poverty is the trouble, go to work on that, and clear it up once and for all. It can be done. If you are unhappy, dissatisfied with your lot, or your surroundings, above all, with yourself, set to work on that; refuse to take "no" for an answer; and insist upon the happiness and satisfaction that are yours by Divine Right.

If your need is self-expression—artistic, literary, or otherwise—if your heart's desire is to attain to eminence in a profession, or some kind of public career, that, too, approached in the right spirit, is a legitimate and worthy object, and the right method of Scientific Prayer will bring you the prize.

Keep a record of your results, and on no account be satisfied with anything less than success. Above all things, avoid the deadly error of making excuses. There are no excuses for failing to demonstrate. When you do not demonstrate, it never by any chance means anything except that you have not worked long enough or in the right way. Excuses are the true and veritable devil who comes to tempt you to remain outside the Kingdom of Heaven, while the Gate stands open. Excuses, in fact, are the only enemy that you really need to fear.

Find the method that suits you; cultivate simplicity— simplicity and spontaneity are the secret of effective prayer —work away steadily; *keep your own counsel; and whatsoever ye shall ask in My name, that will I do.*

The object of treatment is to produce a certain state of mind. That state of mind constitutes a true understanding concerning the problem in question and freedom from fear in connection with it. When this state of mind is attained, the demonstration must and does follow.

Whatever produces the required state of mind is a good treatment. Repeating certain affirmations, reading certain verses in the Bible, using the "Presence Card" or "The Golden Key" or "The Good Shepherd" or any other "method" of producing that state of mind is a good treatment.

Note, however, that using the affirmations or reading spiritual literature is not an end in itself. It is the uplifted state of mind that is the end. Many sincere Christians have come to mistake the means for the end and think that praying mechanically or going through certain forms constitutes the spiritual life; but this is not so. The spiritual life is the search for higher states of consciousness and nothing else. Jesus cautions about vain repetitions.

Whether you be praying to heal a problem (physical or otherwise) or for the general development of your soul, the higher level of understanding is the objective.

Here is one way of solving a problem by Scientific Prayer, or, as we say in metaphysics, of getting a demonstration.

Get by yourself, and be quiet for a few moments. This is very important. Do not strain to think rightly or to find the right thought, etc., but just be quiet. Remind yourself that the Bible says *Be still, and know that I am God.*

Then begin to think about God. Remind yourself of some of the things that you know about Him—that He is present everywhere, that He has all power, that He knows you and loves you and cares for you, and so forth. Read a few verses of the Bible, or a paragraph from any spiritual book that helps you.

During this stage it is important not to think about your problem, *but to give your attention to God.* In other words, do not try to solve your problem directly (which would be using will power) but rather become interested in thinking of the Nature of God.

Then claim the thing that you need—a healing, or some particular good which you lack. Claim it quietly and confidently; as you would ask for something to which you are entitled.

Then give thanks for the accomplished fact; as you would if somebody handed you a gift. Jesus said, "When you pray believe that you receive and you shall receive" (Matt. 21:22). As a matter of fact, Jesus understood the Truth so well that in what might be termed some of his most difficult cases, he made the demonstration by merely giving thanks for the accomplished fact. For instance, in the feeding of the five thousand he kept giving thanks for the supply, and the loaves and fishes kept multiplying. In the raising of Lazarus he said, "Thank thee Father for having heard me," and Lazarus came out of the tomb.

Do not discuss your treatment with anyone.

Try not to be tense or hurried. *Tension and hurry delay the demonstration.* You know that if you try to unlock a door hurriedly, the key is apt to stick, whereas if you do it slowly, it seldom does. If the key sticks, the thing is to stop pressing, take your breath and release it gently. To push hard with will power can only jam the lock completely. So it is with all mental working. *In quietness and confidence shall be your strength.*

I have heard people say, "I did not treat when such a problem arose; I just knew the Truth about it, and the trouble disappeared." But this, of course, is exactly what Scientific Prayer or treatment is, and in its most beautiful and effective form. Such a person really means that he has not used some rigid or crystallized form of expression, which, needless to say, is not in the least essential. Formal or set treatments are useful things to have by one, to fall back upon when spontaneity fails. Then they help to focus the thought, and usually set the natural well abubbling. But—the thought's the thing—and the simpler and more spontaneous it is, and the more quickly it comes, the better.

To know the Truth is really to know that the problem in question does not belong to you as a child of God; that you really have an angel sitting on your shoulder taking care of the whole thing.

It must not be overlooked, however, that very many people actually do all their work with formal statements of Truth, and get consistently good results by working in this way. Not through repeating affirmations like a parrot, needless to say. Those who work like a parrot inevitably make the parrot's demonstration—they remain in the cage. Of a good worker who used the same phrases many times it was said by a friend: "He constantly uses the old affirmations, but he stuffs them with fresh feeling every time." Each prayer must be as fresh as the morning dew.

For one who has neither very much intuitional power at his command, nor yet the ability easily to express his thoughts in words, using affirmations is a model procedure. Meanwhile, in such a case the student must be particularly careful not to accept his want of intuitional power as a fixed thing, but to recognize it merely as a temporary disability to be gradually overcome. In fact, such a person should make a special point of treating himself for intuitional power regularly every day—claiming it, of course—*I have conscious Divine Intelligence. I individualize Omniscience. I have direct knowledge of Truth. I have perfect intuition. I have spiritual perception. I know.*

FAITH

Verily, I say unto you, if ye have faith, and doubt not, ye shall not only do this which is done to the fig tree, but also if ye shall say unto this mountain, be thou removed, and be thou cast into the sea; it shall be done.—Matthew 21:21

An understanding faith is the life of prayer. It is a great mistake, however, to struggle to produce a lively faith within yourself. That can only end in failure. The thing to do is to *act as though you had faith.* What we voluntarily do will always be the expression of our true belief. Act out the part that you wish to demonstrate, and you will be expressing true faith. "Act as though I were, and I will be," says the Bible in effect. This is the right use of the will, scientifically understood.

The statement of Jesus quoted above is perhaps the most tremendous spiritual pronouncement ever made. Probably no other teacher who ever lived would have dared to say it, but Jesus knew the law of faith and proved it himself many times. We shall move mountains (mountains of difficulty, depression, and disappointment) when we are willing to believe that we can, and then not only will mountains be moved, but the whole planet will be redeemed and re-formed according to the Pattern in the Mount.

Know the Truth about your problems. Claim spiritual dominion. Avoid tenseness, strain, and overanxiety. Expect your prayer to be answered, and *act* as though you expected it.

TAKING MATERIAL STEPS

When you set out to solve a problem by means of prayer you should take all the ordinary normal steps in addition. Wise action must be added to prayer. Pray about your difficulty but also claim Divine Guidance, and then take any steps that common sense dictates. We cannot remind ourselves too often that what we call common sense is itself an expression of Divine Wisdom. It is foolish to pray for help while neglecting some obvious and handy stepping-stone.

Many people seem to have the idea that taking some "material" step shows a lack of faith in God and lessens the power of the prayer. They ask if that is not trying to serve two masters.

The exact contrary is the case. We all know that an action is but the outer expression of a thought, and that a wise action is the expression of a wise or true thought, and so to take wise steps is but the proof that one is thinking rightly, and is, indeed, a part of the prayer itself.

Do not simply pray and then sit down and wait for something dramatic to happen. For instance, if you are praying for a position, you should pray for it as well as you know how each day and then go out and visit agencies or prospective employers, write applications, or insert advertisements in suitable periodicals if that is customary in your line of work.

If you want a healing, treat about it in whatever way you usually find to be best and, in addition, take whatever material steps seem to be appropriate. Ask yourself if you are living in accordance with the laws of health, and if not, you must mend your ways at once.

I should point out that when a person came to the office for consultation and spiritual treatment, and if he felt he was suffering with a serious disease, Emmet Fox would ask, "Have you been to a doctor?" Invariably the answer would be, "No, I'm too frightened to go. I am afraid of what he will tell me." Emmet Fox would insist that an examination by a medical doctor be made. He did this not because he had any doubts about a spiritual healing. I witnessed the healing of many diseases, sometimes occurring in a dramatic fashion and later confirmed by a doctor. The purpose of the medical examination was for the patient to learn that the illness often was not so serious as he thought. Once the pressure of intense fear was lifted, the spiritual healing was made much easier. Fear is present in every problem or difficulty.

At this point I should also mention that many doctors sent their patients to Emmet Fox, among them some of the best-known people.

To continue with the question of taking material steps:

If your business is not prospering, treat it, and then have a checkup to discover if you are managing it efficiently, or whether your employees are. If you find weak points in it, as you almost certainly will, you must correct them forthwith.

We certainly cannot expect to go on breaking the laws of the plane on which we live, and expect prayer to compensate for this foolishness.

When you treat for guidance or inspiration, it will often come in the form of your own common-sense answer to the question. What we call "common sense" is just Divine Wisdom taking a particular form.

When we have no idea of what to do, then will be the time to treat for harmony or for guidance, and patiently await our answer, but all obvious and natural steps should always be taken.

REALIZATION

There is a big difference between what you really believe and what you think you ought to believe, or what you want to believe. You actually demonstrate what you really believe, be it good or bad.

It is not much use saying that you know that a thing will not hurt you if you only know it intellectually. If you *realize* even slightly that it cannot hurt you, the case is different.

It is not enough to say that you will be all right, unless you believe it. It is not enough to say that God will take care of you unless you realize and believe what you are saying, to at least a small degree.

The sole object of spiritual treatment is to increase your *realization* of the truth which you already accept; namely that God can and will protect you from all harm, and that fear and error have no power when you yourself do not give it to them.

Realization means to make God absolutely real to yourself as a subconscious conviction. If you can *realize* the Presence of God where previously you were thinking of a damaged organ, for instance, the organ in question will begin to heal. It makes no difference whether you are working for yourself or for someone else, or how far away the other person may be; the law is the same. In practice most people find it easier to heal someone else in this way than themselves, but there is no real reason why this should be the case, and one should practice to overcome this handicap.

The *realization* of God is, of course, a matter of degree. With a sufficient degree of realization the healing will be instantaneous. With a lesser degree it will follow a little later. It is not often, however, that one gets a sufficient degree of realization in one treatment. What happens is that the process is gone through a certain number of times, day after day, as may be required, the patient improving, until at last the healing takes place.

As we progress in Truth we should find that the number of treatments required becomes less and less.

Such a treatment may take only a few seconds, or it may take quite a long time, according to the temperament of the worker, and the particular conditions of the case; but it is not the time that counts, it is the degree of realization attained.

HOW TO MEDITATE EASILY

Truth students are constantly urged to practice meditation on Divine things and, indeed, there is no more powerful form of prayer. It is the Practice of the Presence of God in its most effective form, and is the quickest way out of sin, sickness, and inharmony. But, unfortunately, many people have a fixed idea that they cannot meditate. Now, the fact is that everyone can and does meditate. Even the most seemingly material people constantly meditate—only they do not meditate on Divine things.

Thousands of men meditate deeply upon the subject of baseball during the season, without in the least realizing that they are doing so. What usually happens is something like this: John Smith gets up in the morning, picks up all the problems of his life where he left them before going to sleep; goes down to breakfast and engages in conversation about family matters. On the railroad platform he buys a paper, reads some of the headings on the front page. And then the train comes in. He finds a seat, turns over to the baseball page. Here he reads steadily for ten or fifteen minutes, and now a change takes place. He becomes absorbed in what he is reading; all other subjects fade out of his mind. Home and business troubles, politics, crime, all are forgotten. Presently he lays down the paper and becomes lost in the contemplation of his subject. In his mind he criticizes the management of his favorite team. Possibly he thinks of certain changes which he would like to see made in the rules of the game—and much more along the same line. The next thing he knows, thirty or forty minutes have passed, and he has arrived at his destination.

Here is an excellent example of a first-class meditation— except that it has been about baseball instead of about Divine things. This man read up his subject for ten or fifteen minutes and thus got away from the general stream of thought. Having done this, he proceeded to think through and about his subject until he became absorbed in it—his technique was perfect.

Now, if you will imitate him, except that you will read a spiritual book for ten or fifteen minutes, and think about God—taking perhaps the Seven Main Aspects in turn— think about your spiritual self, think about the Truth of Being in any shape or form, you will have made a wonderful meditation too. And if you do this you cannot fail of remarkable results.

IN TIME OF DANGER

In time of danger, the best prayer or treatment is to be aware of the protecting power of God's Love. Where the danger is immediate, a short treatment, like *God is here* or *God is with me*, will suffice because the urgency of the problem gives more spiritual weight to the treatment. There have been many cases where someone has slipped or tripped, and this simple treatment has brought them out unscathed.

A case in mind is that of a very large woman who at the time was wearing a long dress. As she went down the subway steps, her heel caught in the hem of the dress, and over she went. She had only time to say, "God is helping me; God is helping me!" when she arrived at the bottom of the steps. People ran over to help her up. No damage to her person; only perhaps to her dignity. Even her dress was not damaged; slightly soiled.

In time of what seems impending danger, where there is time to treat, the 91st Psalm* should be used, over and

*See "The Secret Place" in *Power Through Constructive Thinking*.

over, if need be. This psalm covers all sorts of situations, sometimes symbolically, and is summed up in the thought, "He shall give his angels charge over thee."

*A case of this sort involving Emmet Fox and the author will be found in the biographical section of this book.**

In all your spiritual work, whether prayer, treatment, or meditation, have a quiet confidence that because you are contacting God, God is answering, and then remind yourself that you really do have an angel on your shoulder.

* P. 220.

The
Word of
Power

The Word of Power is in itself a golden key, for as Emmet Fox points out, it opens the door to abundant and successful living. It is the basic idea in the whole scheme of creation. As Jesus understood it and as Emmet Fox taught it, the Word refers to any definitely formulated thought with the essence of God in it.

John, who probably understood the inner teaching of Jesus better than any of the other disciples, begins his treatise, "In the beginning was the Word, and the Word was with God, and the Word was God" (John 1:1). This is the Logos, the creative Word—in Greek. John's statement ties in with the very beginning of the Bible—the Seven Days of Creation.*

You will note that God says, "Let there be"—and there was. Let there be Light and light appeared. Let there be a Firmament, and the firmament comes into being. It is the

*See *Alter Your Life.*

basic idea behind creation. It tells how everything is created whether it be by the Mind of God or the mind of man.

Everything begins with thought. God did not have a stack of planets and stars to choose from and then set them in the firmament. If that were the case there would have been a prior creation. No, it was purely a mental action— let there be. In other words, it was the expression of an idea—the Word—in the Mind of God. We say the Mind of God but actually God is Mind—and there is nothing else.

Jesus understood this idea, this process, so completely that he could speak the Word once, and the healing, the demonstration of prosperity, etc., occurred immediately.

Jesus was surprised when the Roman centurion—a heathen in the eyes of the Hebrews—came to him for the healing of his servant who lay at death's door. When Jesus said to him, "I will come and heal him," this Roman commander had sufficient understanding of how Jesus healed, that he replied, "Speak the Word only, and my servant shall be healed." And Jesus, recognizing the great faith and understanding of this centurion, said, "Go thy way, and as thou hast believed, so be it done unto thee." And we are told that the servant was healed in the selfsame hour.

This is a very clear case of the spiritual healing process. But the same idea was at work in all of the healings of Jesus. This is the Word of Power as Jesus taught it and demonstrated it. It is the Word that Isaiah, one of the greatest of prophets, spoke:

"So shall my word be that goeth forth out of my mouth; it shall not return unto me void, but it shall accomplish that which I please, and it shall prosper in the thing whereto I sent it" (Isa. 55:11).

Emmet Fox was deeply conscious of speaking the Word and used it often, sometimes with dramatic results. He was able to "clear his mind," as he said, "of the difficulty," and then the healing was accomplished. I have been witness to a number of these healings, on occasion at the bedside of a hospital patient.

The ability to speak the Word of Power is not just a matter of making a few affirmations but has to be built up over a period of time through prayer and meditation. Jesus was a praying man and often went up into the mountains to recharge his spiritual batteries, as Paul did when he went out into the wilderness for a few years to clear his thought. Moses could never have accomplished his mission without steady communion with God. Emmet Fox, too, spent hours in prayer and meditation, not just for a healing or other demonstration but to make his connection with God.

For those who wanted to increase their prayer power, he recommended this golden key as a daily spiritual excercise, what he called "The Word of Power":*

I am Divine Spirit. In God I live, and move, and have my being. I am part of the self-expression of God, and I therefore express perfect harmony. I individualize Omniscience. I have direct knowledge of Truth. I have perfect intuition. I have spiritual perception. I know.

God is my Wisdom; so I cannot err. God is my Intelligence; so I am always thinking rightly. There is no waste of time, for God is the only Doer. God works through me; so I am always working rightly, and there is no danger of my praying wrongly.

*See *Power Through Constructive Thinking.*

I think the right thing, in the right way, at the right time. My work is always well done, for my work is God's work. The Holy Spirit is continually inspiring me. My thoughts are fresh, and new, and clear, and powerful with the might of Omnipotence. My prayers are the handiwork of the Holy Ghost—powerful as the eagle and gentle as the dove. They go forth in the name of God Himself, and they cannot return unto me void. They shall accomplish that which I please, and prosper in the thing whereto I send them. I thank God for this.

The idea behind this daily exercise is to establish in the subconscious the belief that one actually has the power of the spoken Word, and continued use of this daily prayer will help to do just that.

While Emmet Fox in his own life and in his teaching followed the dictum, "Use no formulas—let God lead," he also understood that on occasion, especially in times of great stress, the mind of the particular individual might be too full of fear to formulate anything but more negativity. Consequently he realized the value of having certain affirmations and set treatments for ready use.

One of the treatments often used by him at services and meetings is called "Now I Speak the Word."* I have simply changed it from the second person to the first:

God is Infinite Life. God is Boundless Love. God is Infinite Intelligence. God is Unfathomable Wisdom. God is Unspeakable Beauty. God is the Unchanging Principle of Perfect Good. God is the Soul of man.

*See *Stake Your Claim.*

I am the image and likeness of God, and I have the power of the Word. When I speak that Word, it goes forth and cannot return void. It accomplishes the thing whereunto I send it. That Word goes forth charged with the power of God.

Now I speak the Word in my name————. I invoke the power of the Healing Christ, and I say that the full power of God is now awakened in me, filling my soul with peace and life and joy. God is Light and that Light fills my soul. My soul is as the burning bush that burned with the power of God and was not consumed. There are no dark corners left; no complexes or neuroses, no fears or doubts; no old dark things. God is Light and in Him there is no darkness at all.

God is Life and that Life builds every cell in my body. The tide of Divine Life sweeps through my body, carrying before It any toxins, any foreign things that should not be there. It reforms, re-creates, regenerates every organ and tissue, and charges it with Its own Divine Life.

I claim that the peace of God surrounds me and fills me. That peace goes with me as a pillar of cloud by day and a pillar of fire by night. In that peace, and that health, and that harmony I dwell.

I claim that the power of God goes before me and makes my path straight. It opens my way for true prosperity, for freedom, for unlimited spiritual growth.

I claim that God is bringing into my life the right people that I can be of service to and who can help me; and that those who wish me ill will fade out of my life and prosper elsewhere.

I claim that all that God is, is now working to move me into my true place. The outer thing is but a picture, and the power of God is changing that picture now and moving me into my true place.

One Presence . . . One Power . . . One Mind. One God
. . . One Law . . . One Element. I am part of that Divine
Presence and in that Presence I dwell forever.

And I believe that according to my faith will it be done
unto me.

*This prayer can be used as a daily meditation until
the subconscious becomes thoroughly saturated with
the spiritual ideas involved. There will come a time
when you will know that they are true for you and in
you, and you will speak the Word with authority. In
the meantime, any of the clauses or paragraphs can be
used as an affirmation in a particular case.*

Your
Success
Story

Perhaps in time the many healings and the down-to-earth yet highly spiritual instruction of Emmet Fox will be forgotten as new generations come upon the scene, but what will be a lasting tribute to his work, a golden key to those yet unborn, is his unveiling of the Bible.

As early as his first lecture in New York he awakened his listeners to the immense and practical value of the Bible in their lives. He instructed everyone to write on the first page of the Bible, in large letters, "THIS MEANS ME." Then go on to the first four words in the Bible, "In the beginning, God," and realize that God should be the beginning of every enterprise in life.

Countless people have told me that before they heard Emmet Fox speak of it, they held the Bible as a sacred book but thought it rather dull reading and at times unbelievable. Often the Bible was little more than a dust collector on a shelf or desk. One recalls the story of the lady who was ill and visited by the local minister. After talking with her for a little

*while, he asked, "Do you have a Bible in the house?"
The lady replied, "I wouldn't be without one," and
called to her young son, "Johnny, bring mama that
book she loves so much!" And Johnny appeared
carrying the Sears Roebuck catalog.*

*Emmet Fox changed all that for millions of people.
I remember one fine Jewish woman, a member of
Temple Emanu-El on Fifth Avenue, saying that she
never understood her own religion until she heard
Emmet Fox's explanation of the Scriptures. She never
quite realized that Abraham stood for rational faith
and so had never grasped the amazing accomplish-
ments that faith had wrought. She said that for her
Moses became a real person with a vast knowledge of
the true God; and that she even gained a better
understanding of Jesus Christ.*

*Roman Catholics attended mass first and then
came to the meetings. Not only did members of every
religious persuasion attend, but many ministers of
the various faiths as well.*

*In 1934 Harper & Brothers (now Harper & Row)
published Emmet Fox's interpretation of* The Sermon on the Mount, *which immediately became a
bestseller among religious books and has remained
one ever since. It has become a religious classic, a
basic textbook not only in the metaphysical movement, but has been used in many of the orthodox
churches as well.*

*Under Emmet Fox's inspiration and deep under-
standing, Jesus' famous Sermon on the Mount becomes a golden key to successful modern living. The
seemingly obscure and contradictory teaching—as,
for example, Jesus' precept to resist not evil—be-*

comes vital, usable instruction in handling life's difficult problems.

A few years ago a young accountant came to see me to share his experience with The Sermon on the Mount. He was having a tough time at his office, not receiving the remuneration nor the promotion he felt he was entitled to. As a consequence he felt his wife and child were suffering, and there was a good deal of friction at home. Try as he would, the situation showed no improvement. But God works in mysterious ways. Walking out of the subway one morning on his way to the office, he saw a book in a bookshop window whose subtitle read, "The Key to Success in Life." He murmured, "That's surely what I need." But as he read the title, The Sermon on the Mount, his spirits dropped, for, alas, he was of Jewish persuasion, and he thought a book about Jesus was just a little too much. But his route to the office took him past that bookshop every morning, and daily he read the subtitle, "The Key to Success in Life." At last he could no longer resist. He bought the book, but now he had another problem. He did not dare bring the book home for fear of offending his wife who was even more committed to the Jewish religion than he was. So he decided to read the book during his lunch hours and keep it in his desk. He read it and reread it, and admitted the greatest difficulty for him was to accept the name Jesus Christ. But in the end the book literally transformed his life. It was not long before he had a new job with substantial income increase, and eventually all the difficulty at home disappeared.

Another case of the power of the Emmet Fox teaching was that of a husband and wife who were finally *persuaded to come to the meetings. One Wednesday evening they bought a copy of* The Sermon on the Mount. *Reading and rereading it completely changed their lives, and they got what had always been in their hearts, a ranch out west. Acting on their hunch, they settled in Idaho and became successful ranchers.*

Such is the power of The Sermon on the Mount, *now published in French, Spanish, Greek, German, and Portuguese. Countless letters have come in from people in all walks of life and of every religious bent, testifying to completely changed lives.*

Emmet Fox continues his unfolding of the Bible as a source of practical power with his Power Through Constructive Thinking, *which, among other topics, gives the inner meaning of a number of the Psalms.*

In Emmet Fox's The Ten Commandments, *Moses' rules of conduct—"Thou shalt not . . ."—take on a new constructive meaning, as the individual is led to realize that he does not have to take anything from anyone, indeed cannot, but that all things are his "by right of consciousness" only.*

In 1968 Emmet Fox's Diagrams for Living *was published and in it he reveals that "the Bible is really a grand diagram of man's destiny."*

After you have come through the trials and the tribulations, the successes and the triumphs of life, you emerge as the woman clothed with the sun. The moon is under your feet, and upon your head is a crown of twelve stars. You realize that you were born to be free, you have caught the spiritual vision. You are ready to triumph over every challenge, for at long last you know that you are a jewel in the diadem of God. No longer do you have to be blown by the winds of "fate." You are the seven times seven, the twelve times twelve, the measure of a man.

> *And Emmet Fox closes with an explanation of some of the most complicated symbolism to be found anywhere in occult literature—the Book of Revelation of Jesus Christ hmself given to John.*
>
> *Let us see some of the things Emmet Fox says about the Bible, and your success story.*

The Bible is the most precious possession of the human race. It contains the key to life. It shows us how to live so that we may have health, freedom, and prosperity. It meets everyone on his own level and brings him to God. It has a solution for every problem. Incidentally, it is the greatest literary work ever compiled, and by far the most interesting of all books. Our common version (King James) contains the greatest and finest English ever written.

Nevertheless, the real value of the Bible lies in the spiritual interpretation. Wonderful as the "outer" Bible is, it is far less than one percent of the "inner" Bible—the Bible that is hidden behind the symbols. If you have been reading the Bible without the spiritual interpretation, you have not found the real message of the Bible, for that lies below the surface. The outer Bible is wonderful, but *the inner Bible is the supreme gift of God.* "Ye do err, not knowing the scriptures" (Matt. 22:19).

The Bible is not primarily intended to teach history, or biography, or natural science. It is intended to teach psychology and metaphysics. It deals basically with states of mind and the laws of mental activity; and anything else is only incidental. Each of the principal characters in the Bible represents a state of mind that any of us may experience; and the events that happen to the various characters illustrate the consequences to us of entertaining such states of mind, either good or bad.

Some of the Bible characters, such as Moses, Elijah, and Paul, are historical figures. They were real men who lived on earth and did the deeds attributed to them; nonetheless they represent states of mind also, and, in turn, they out-pictured different states of mind at different times as their lives unfolded. Other Bible characters, such as Adam and Eve, the Prodigal Son, the Good Samaritan (Luke 10:33), or the Scarlet Woman (Rev. 17:3–4), are, of course, fictional and never had an actual existence; but they express states of mind too, and always in a remarkably simple and graphic manner.

The leading events in the Bible describe the consequences following upon certain states of mind. His faith and understanding get Moses out of Egypt (Exod. 14:21), and get Peter out of prison (Acts 12:7), and these qualities will liberate anyone else in the same way, whether it be a prison of sin, of fear, of doubt, or some other human limitation.

Now a state of mind cannot be viewed or pictured directly as can a material object. It can only be described indirectly, by a figure of speech, an allegory, or a parable, but, unfortunately, thoughtless people have always tended to take the figure of speech or the allegory literally, at its face value, thus missing the real meaning, because it lies hidden beneath. The veil of Isis comes to be worshiped while Isis herself is forgotten. Another evil that follows from this course is that, since many parables obviously *cannot* be literally true, such people, unable to accept the authenticity of the story, proceed to reject the Bible altogether as a collection of falsehoods or myths. This was the attitude of Ingersoll in America, Bradlaugh in England, and many others. The fundamentalist, on the other hand, does violence to his common sense in trying to make himself believe that these parables are literally true, while at the bottom of his heart—which is the place that matters—he cannot really believe them, and so a dangerous conflict is set up within his subconscious.

Any text in the Bible can be taken in the present, the past, or the future tense—because God is outside of time.

The heroes of the Bible are represented as having many faults in the beginning (Moses killed a man before he got his enlightenment and Paul stoned the early Christians while his name was yet Saul), but each gradually overcame these faults by much prayer and fasting. And this is very encouraging for us.

The Bible teaches that outer conditions and events are not important in themselves, but only insofar as they necessarily express the character (consciousness) of the subject.

The Bible is infinitely *optimistic* but never Pollyanna. It does not say that "everything will be all right." Things will not be all right unless you make them so by right thinking. It teaches that negative thoughts and beliefs, especially the sin of limiting God (Ps. 78:41), can bring all kinds of trouble and suffering in their train. Wrong thinking can only bring wrong results.

It is not a *get rich quick* scheme. It teaches that if you have faith in God, He will supply your needs bountifully; but metaphysics will not bring money for its own sake.

It does not teach that you have only to *order what you want*—by thinking it—and that God must obey your orders. This absurd idea usually ends in disaster. The Truth is that you can demonstrate only what you really have the consciousness for; and what you have the consciousness for you must demonstrate.

It is not *mind over matter*. It teaches that what we see

around us is but our own thoughts and beliefs objectified. Thus we do not try to dominate something outside of our minds, but to change our minds.

It does not pretend that your *trouble is imaginary*. It admits that it is there as an experience; but it says that that experience can be dissolved by realizing the Presence of God.

It is not *faith healing* in the ordinary sense of fighting a supposedly real evil with blind faith and will power. It teaches an intelligent and understanding Faith based on the goodness and all-presence of God.

It is not *Pantheism*. Pantheism, as generally understood, gives the outer world a separate and substantial existence and says that it is part of God—including all the evil and cruelty to be found in it. The truth is that God is the only Presence and the only Power, that He is entirely good, that evil is a false belief about the Truth, and that the outer world is the outpicturing of our own minds.

The Bible teaches that *today's prayer can put everything right*—if only you will not look back to yesterday. Remember Lot's wife. She turned into a pillar of salt. Salt is a preservative and in the Bible symbolizes that tenacious holding on to the past which keeps one chained to the old conditions, while the Bible teaches us to go forward with new ideas and new aspirations, to new adventures.

Do not postpone reading the Bible until you "have plenty of time and can do it thoroughly," but start today and read a little—even a few verses—daily.

And in order to do that with greater understanding, Emmet Fox gives us some key words in the Bible—words that not only open up the Bible but open up our lives as well.

FEAR

The Bible says that the fear of the Lord is the beginning of wisdom (Ps. 111:10) and the beginning of knowledge (Prov. 1:7). This has misled many people, because the truth is that fear is entirely evil and is indeed the only enemy we have. You can heal any condition if you can get rid of the fear attaching to it. Trouble or sickness is nothing but subconscious fear outpictured in our surroundings. It is true at all times that "we have nothing to fear but fear."

How then do we account for the texts quoted? The answer is that in the Bible the fear of God means *reverence* for God, not fear in the usual sense of the word.

Reverence for God is the beginning of wisdom. How do we show reverence for God? Not by fine professions or sanctimonious prayers, but by seeing God everywhere, refusing to recognize anything unlike Him, and by living the Christ life.

Confidence is worship. You worship whatever you trust. Are you trusting more in evil or in good? in fear or in God? What are you worshiping? That is the test.

"Acquaint now thyself with Him, and be at peace" (Job 22:21).

WRATH

There are many references in the Bible to the wrath of God. This puzzles many students of metaphysics because we know that God is Love and that the action of God always takes place to heal, to comfort, and to inspire. The explanation is that the word "wrath" in the Bible really means *great activity*—the activity that accompanies or precedes the healing of any negative condition. We know that while the spring cleaning of a house is in progress everything seems to be turned upside down for a few days. Also, when you heal a sick person by prayer he frequently gets worse before the healing comes. This kind of crisis is what is signified by "wrath."

In II Chronicles 34:25, for instance, we are told that the wrath of the Lord will be poured out upon the people because they have worshiped false gods. This means that when we believe in limitation and entertain negative thoughts, trouble must follow, but that if we treat, our treatment will undo the harm done and bring peace and harmony into our lives. This activity is the wrath of God.

Habakkuk's prayer (Hab. 3:2) illustrates the mental anguish that often accompanies the activity (wrath) of God in our souls, when difficulties come to the surface to be cleared, and a period of stress comes before the demonstration.

In Psalm 76:10 it says, "The wrath of men shall praise thee." This means again that the stirring up in us caused by our troubles leads us to turn to God and in that way overcome them.

The Bible always presents trouble and misfortune as ending in harmony and joy if we will turn to God.

"He sent His word, and healed them, and delivered them from their destructions" (Ps. 107:20).

I AM THAT I AM

I AM THAT I AM (Exod. 3:14) is one of the principal Bible terms for God. It means unconditioned Being. It means the great Creative Power that is absolutely unlimited. It is an attempt—and a very successful one—to express, as far as language can, the infinity of God.

"I AM" means you—the individual. It is an assertion or affirmation of existence and needs to be qualified in some way. We say, for example, "I am a man" or "I am a

woman," or "I am an American" or "I am a Spaniard," "I
am a lawyer" or "I am a baker." In each case we state an
important fact about ourselves, and to that extent we limit
ourselves—not in a negative sense, but in a positive and
constructive sense. If I am an American, I am not a Spaniard; if I am a man, I am not a woman, etc.

Now God is absolutely unlimited, and the only phrase
which can express this is I AM THAT I AM. I AM—what?
I AM—pure unconditioned being, unlimited, and unspe-
cified in any way. To affirm that God is any particular
thing would imply limitation, or at least a circumscription,
and God is unlimited.

It is man's business to be something in particular, and
not to try to be everything, because he is an *individualization.* If you struck all the notes in the scale together you
would only have confused noise. Music consists in the selection and special groupings of certain notes.

In God's universe each one of us has his place and it
is our business to find that true place and express it—to
play our part correctly in the great orchestra. God, however, is the Great Conductor and the whole orchestra too,
unlimited and without end.*

SALVATION

The word "salvation" appears more than 120 times in
the Bible. It was in constant use among religious people of
past generations, and while it is not so often heard today,
the fact remains that it is one of the most important words
in the Bible, and, as so often happens, it is among the least
well understood.

*See booklet, "Life Is Consciousness," published by Unity School of
Christianity, Unity Village, Mo. 64065.

The word "salvation," in the Bible, means perfect health, harmony, and freedom. When you have a strong healthy body so that just to be alive is a joy in itself; when you are living in conditions that are completely harmonious; when your time is filled with joyous and useful activities; when you are increasing daily in understanding of God, and are not conscious of any fear—you have salvation in the Bible sense.

These things are the will of God for man—for you personally; and the Bible was written to tell us how to attain them.

We gain salvation by seeking God in thought and letting Him work through us; by refusing to give power to outer conditions; by training ourselves to despise fear.

"The Lord is my light and my salvation" (Ps. 27:1). He only is my rock and my salvation" (Ps. 62:2). He hath raised an horn of salvation for us" (Luke 1:69). All flesh shall see the salvation of God" (Luke 3:6). Such texts as these are typical of the Bible promises concerning salvation.

Salvation comes to a few people gently and easily, but the majority have to work out their salvation with a certain amount of "fear and trembling" for the time being. The actual way in which it comes is not really important, for come it will—when we seek it with our whole heart.

It is an excellent treatment to look up the word "salvation" in a concordance, and then read a number of the verses containing it, interpreting them spiritually of course.

WICKED

The word "wicked" occurs more than three hundred times in the Bible and is one of the most important terms to be found therein. In the Bible the word "wicked" really means "bewitched" or "under a spell." The Law of Being is perfect harmony and that truth never changes; but man uses his free will to think wrongly, and thus he builds up false conditions around him, and then believes them to be real. They look real, and so he forgets that it was he himself who made them, and thus he bewitches himself, or throws himself under a kind of spell; and of course as long as he remains bewitched in this way he has to suffer the consequences. Nevertheless, it is only illusion, or a spell, and it can be broken by turning to God.

That is why Jesus called it the strait and narrow way. "Oh foolish Galatians, who hath bewitched you?" (Gal. 3:1) said Paul when he heard that some of his students had begun to believe in evil in this way.

"The wicked flee when no man pursueth" (Prov. 28:1). "The wicked shall be turned into hell" (Ps. 9:17). "Let the wicked forsake his way, and the unrighteous man his thoughts: and let him return unto the Lord, and He will have mercy upon him" (Isa. 55:7). These are all statements of what happens when we allow ourselves to be bewitched by our own thoughts into believing in any power other than God. We flee when no man pursueth—we are afraid of things without reason. We can suffer the pains of hell because "fear hath torment"—but when we turn to God, the spell is broken and harmony is restored.

Let us awaken from the spell under which the whole race lives, and know instead that God is all Power, infinite Intelligence, and boundless Love.

JUDGMENT

Judgment, in the Bible, means deciding upon the truth or falsity of any thought. This process necessarily goes on in our minds all the time we are awake, and the extent to which we "judge righteous judgments" determines the character of our lives. To accept evil at its face value is to judge wrongly, and bring its natural punishment. To decline to believe in evil, and to affirm the good, is righteous judgment and brings the reward of happiness and harmony.

Thus *The Judgment* is not a great trial to take place at the end of time; it is a process that goes on every day. When Jesus said, "Judge not, that ye be not judged" (Matt. 7:1), he meant that to condemn our brother out of hand instead of seeing the Christ within him, is to put ourselves in danger, because we are making a reality of those appearances in him, and whatever we make real we must demonstrate in *our own* lives.

HEATHENS, ENEMIES, STRANGERS

These mean your own negative thoughts, which are the things that are causing your difficulties. They do not mean other human beings. Wrong thoughts are *heathens* because they do not know God. They are *strangers* to your real self, and of course, they are the only *enemies* that you can have. All such enemies are to be destroyed, not by wrestling with them which only gives them power, but by righteous *judgment*—refusing to believe in them.

God is the only Presence and the only Power.

CHRIST

The word "Christ" is not a proper name. It is a title. It is a Greek word meaning anointed or consecrated. It corresponds somewhat to the Hebrew term Messiah, and to the oriental word Buddha.

Jesus was the personal name given to our Lord by his

parents. The word, as we have it, is Greek and is a translation of the Hebrew Joshua, which means, literally, "God is salvation"—that is to say, the realization of God is our salvation, or what I call the Golden Key.

Thus we speak of *the Christ*. The Christ may be defined as the spiritual Truth about any person, situation, or thing. When you realize the spiritual Truth about any problem you are lifting up the Christ in consciousness, and the healing follows. Thus the Christ is always the healing Christ.

Jesus demonstrated the Christ in his own person and life to a greater extent than any other individual who has ever lived on this earth; and because the work that he did in his crucifixion and resurrection has made it possible for us to reach spiritual heights that would otherwise have been quite out of our reach, he is justly termed the Messiah or Savior of the world. For the same reason he is termed the Light of the world. The realization of the Christ heals, irrespective of any conditions or limitation that may seem to stand in the way.

"And I, if I be lifted up from the earth, will draw all men unto me" (John 12:32).

REPENTANCE

To repent means really to change one's mind concerning something. When a person realizes that a particular action, or a certain line of conduct, or perhaps the whole direction of his life, has been wrong, and honestly resolves to change his conduct, he has repented.

The Bible makes true repentance an essential condition for any spiritual progress, and for the forgiveness of sin. Jesus said, "Except ye repent, ye shall all likewise perish" (Luke 13:3).

Repentance does not mean grieving for past mistakes, because this is dwelling in the past, and our duty is to dwell in the present and make this moment right. Worrying over past mistakes is remorse, and remorse is a sin, for it is a refusal to accept God's forgiveness. The Bible says that *now* is the day of salvation.

John the Baptist said, "Repent ye: for the kingdom of heaven is at hand" (Matt. 3:2). This means that you should change your thought and know that the Presence of God is where you are.

John practiced baptism as a symbol of repentance. In his day it was already a very ancient custom among different peoples, because washing or bathing the body is a dramatic symbol of the cleansing of the soul by repentance. In the Old Testament the people washed their clothes before receiving the Ten Commandments from Moses, and in many other cases a ceremonial washing or cleansing preceded various spiritual exercises. This is the real significance of baptism and, of course, the ceremony itself is of no importance except as an expression in the outer of that change of mind, or repentance, or determination to do better, which is the inner and spiritual thing.

The law of life is to know the Truth and live it.

VENGEANCE

"Vengeance is mine; I will repay, saith the Lord" (Rom. 12:19). The spiritual meaning of the word *vengeance*, in the Bible, is *vindication*. It stands for the vindication of Truth against the challenge or accusation of fear and misunderstanding.

We know that the real nature of Being is perfect, unchanging harmony. This is absolute Truth, and nothing can change it. Of course, it is possible for us to accept mistaken ideas about the Truth, and as long as we do accept such mistakes we have to live in their bondage. We also entertain fear, and fear is nothing but a lack of trust in God.

Then, at last, we decide to pray by turning to God and realizing the Truth as well as we can. As soon as we do this, the action of God begins to take place, our fear begins to evaporate, and the false condition is seen improving steadily.

Thus the Truth of Being and the goodness of God are *vindicated* once more in our lives.

When we seem to have received an injury from others, we must, instead of dwelling upon it with resentment, drive all thought of the matter out of our minds by realizing the goodness and harmony of God in ourselves and the delinquent. This is *vindication* or spiritual "vengeance" as the Bible teaches it; and it not only heals the whole condition but brings great spiritual progress to ourselves.

LIFE

Jesus said that he had come that we might have *life*, and that we might have it more abundantly (John 10:10). The Bible often uses the word *life*, and always with the implication that it is the greatest of all blessings. "With long *life* will I satisfy him" (Ps. 91:16). Thou wilt show me the path of *life*" (Ps. 16:11). "Keep thy heart with all diligence, for out of it are the issues of *life*" (Prov. 4:23). Jesus says that those who follow him shall have the light of *life*. And the great goal of man is said all through the Bible to be *eternal life*.

Now what is this life of which the Bible speaks? Well, we shall not attempt to define the word in this little essay. It will be sufficient to point out that you experience *life* only when you are happy, and feel yourself to be free and useful and joyous, and unconscious of either fear or doubt.

Everyone has known such periods in his life, though they are much rarer than they should be, and those are the times that you were alive—that you enjoyed *life*. At other times you did not have *life*, in the Scripture sense.

So when the Bible promises us long life, under certain conditions, it promises us a long period of joy and freedom. When it promises *eternal life*, it promises the enjoyment of these things forever.

A long physical life full of struggle, suffering, and disappointment, living to an advanced age without joy or hope, is not long life in the Bible sense. Such a history is really a form of death.

Life in the Bible sense is something supremely worth having, and we are promised it on the condition that we keep the Great Law—by seeking more knowledge of God, and putting Him first in our lives.

Psychology

As Emmet Fox has pointed out, the Bible teaches psychology and metaphysics; and psychology means the science of mind—how the mind works. Now, there is only one Mind in the universe, the Mind of God, and the human mind is part of that. As Jesus reiterated so many times, "It is the Father within that doeth the work." He was very conscious of the tremendous potential inherent in each one of us. So an understanding of the human mind and how it works is of immense value in every endeavor.

It was natural for Emmet Fox to give his attention to this fundamental expression of God, and here is another of the precious golden keys. To bring our minds up to date he calls our attention to new names for old things.

Modern psychology has done good work in throwing new light on many aspects of the human mind, and thus helping us to understand ourselves better. Naturally, it cannot take the place of prayer, but still it has its uses.

We need to know something of how the human mind

works in order that we may redeem it. It is well, however, to remember that we have always known a good deal about it in general; and we should avoid being confused or intimidated by modern psychological terminology. For the most part, this is but giving new names to old things. The new names are often more precise and instructive, but the things they refer to are things that we have always known about.

We have always known, for instance, that at any given time we are conscious only of a certain number of ideas, of the things that we are doing and thinking about at the moment—and these represent what psychology calls "the conscious mind."

We have always been aware that we know a great many things about which we are not thinking at any given time, some of which we have completely forgotten, but which might be brought back by some unexpected incident; and this is what psychology calls "the subconscious or unconscious mind."

We have always known that we have a tendency to fool ourselves by thinking that we act from one motive when the fact is that we are acting from quite a different one; and this is "rationalization."

We have always known that human nature is very ingenious in inventing some illicit scheme to evade an unpleasant duty or to avoid facing up to an unwelcome fact— and this is "the escape mechanism."

And so on with most of the technical terms of present-day psychology. The important thing is to make sure that when we use them they are our servants and not our masters.

Of course, the one thing that matters is to get a better knowledge of God, and of ourselves, and any study and any experience that helps toward that end is good. "Acquaint now thyself with Him, and be at peace" (Job 22:21).

Since prayer is the most important activity that mind can indulge in it is interesting to know how prayer works. This is what actually happens: Your prayer works by changing the subconscious part of your mind. It wipes out fear, and destroys the false ideas that have been causing the trouble.

Every condition in your life is the outpicturing of a belief in the subconscious. Every ailment, every difficulty that you have, is but the embodiment of a negative idea somewhere in your subconscious, which is actuated by a charge of fear. Prayer wipes out these negative thoughts and then their embodiment must disappear too. The healing must come. This explains too why in many cases a number of prayers or treatments have to be given in order for the subconscious to accept the new and constructive ideas.

Prayer, then, does not act directly on your body or on your circumstances; it changes your mentality—after which, of course, the outer picture must change too.

Paul says, "Be not conformed to this world [the negative picture]: but be ye transformed by the renewing of your mind" (Rom. 12:2).

Thoughtless people sometimes say that our affirmations and meditations are foolish because we state what is not so. "To claim that my body is well or being healed when it is not, is only to tell a lie," said one distinguished man some years ago. But the Bible itself does not agree with him. It says, "Let the weak say I am strong" (Joel 3:10). Is it suggesting using a falsehood? No, the Bible understands the psychology of prayer.

We affirm the harmony that we seek in order to provide the subconscious with a blueprint of the work to be done. When you decide to build a house, you purchase a vacant piece of ground and then your architect prepares drawings of a complete house. Actually, of course, there is no such house on the lot today but you would not think of saying that the architect was drawing a lie. He is drawing what is to be. So, we build in thought the conditions that will later come into manifestation on the physical plane.

To wait like Mr. Micawber for things to "turn up" is foolish, because you will probably die before they do so. What is your intelligence for, if not to be used in building the kind of life you want?

The time has come when intelligent men and women must understand the laws of Mind, and plant consciously the crops that they desire; and just as carefully pull up the weeds that they do not want.

There are a few great laws that govern all thinking, just as there are a few fundamental laws in chemistry, in physics, and in mechanics, for example.

We know that control is the Key of Destiny, and in order to learn thought control we have to know and understand these laws, just as the chemist has to understand the laws of chemistry, and the electrician has to know the laws of electricity.

THE LAW OF SUBSTITUTION

One of the great mental laws is the Law of *Substitution*. This means that the only way to get rid of a certain thought is to substitute another one for it. You cannot dismiss a thought directly. You can do so only by substituting another one for it. On the physical plane this is not the case. You can drop a book or a stone by simply opening your hand and letting it go; but with thought this will not work. If you want to dismiss a negative thought, the only way to do so is to think of something positive and constructive. It is as though in order, let us say, to drop a pencil, it were necessary to put a pen or a book or a stone into your hand when the pencil would fall away.

If I say to you, "Do not think of the Statue of Liberty," of course you immediately think of it. If you say to yourself, "I am not going to think of the Statue of Liberty," that is thinking of it.

> *Apropos of this particular golden key of Emmet Fox's is an interesting story about Tolstoy when he was a boy. He and his brothers played many games together, most of which were invented by his older brother Nicholas. One of these revolved around the idea of finding the secret of happiness. Nicholas told them that the secret of happiness was written on a green stick that was hidden in the ravine, and if one of them found the green stick he must share its secret with the others. However, certain steps had to be taken. First they must band together under the table in the kitchen and swear eternal brotherhood, and next each must stand in a corner and* not *think of a great white bear. Of course, none of them ever found the green stick and its secret of happiness because none of them could stop thinking of a great white bear while standing in the corner.*
>
> *The great law of* Substitution *was inversely at work.*
>
> *Emmet Fox continues his discourse by saying:*

You can only change your thought by becoming interested in something else, say, by turning on the radio, and then you forget all about the Statue of Liberty—or *the great white bear*—and this is a case of *substitution.*

When negative thoughts come to you, do not fight them,

but think of something constructive. Preferably think of God, but if that is difficult at the moment, think of any positive or constructive idea, and then the negative thought will fade out.

It sometimes happens that negative thoughts seem to besiege you in such force that you cannot overcome them. That is what is called a fit of depression, or a fit of worry, or perhaps even a fit of anger. In such a case the best thing is to go and find someone to talk to on any subject, or to go to a good movie or play, or read an interesting book, say a good novel or biography or travel book. If you sit down to fight the negative tide you will probably succeed only in amplifying it.

Turn your attention to something quite different, refusing steadfastly to think of or rehearse the difficulty, and later on, after you have completely gotten away from it, you can come back with confidence and handle it by spiritual treatment. "I say unto you that you resist not evil" (Matt. 5:39).

THE LAW OF RELAXATION

Another of the great mental laws is the Law of *Relaxation*. In all mental working *effort defeats itself*. The more effort you make the less will your result be. This of course is just the opposite of what we find on the physical plane, but it will not surprise us because we know that in many cases the laws of mind are the reverse of the laws of matter.

On the physical plane, usually the more effort we make the greater the result. The harder you press a drill the faster will it go through a plank. The harder you work digging the ground the sooner do you have a ditch. The exact opposite, however, is the case with thought.

Any attempt at mental pressure is foredoomed to failure

because the moment tension begins, the mind stops working creatively, and just runs along on whatever the old habit pattern is. When you try to force things mentally, when you try to hurry mentally, you simply stop your creative power. To enable your mind to become creative again you must un-tense it by consciously relaxing.

Many creative people have found the truth of this. Alfred Tennyson was one who thought that his creative life had come to an abrupt end, until one day he walked out into the quiet of the woods and found "there are sermons in brooks and stones and everything." Emmet Fox also found this to be so. There were times when the printer was breathing down our necks for the essay that was to appear on the back of the next Sunday's program, and I would mention it to him. He would treat a moment, and then say, "No, the well has run dry." But perhaps twenty minutes later after a period of rest and spiritual treatment the "well" would be working splendidly again.

In all mental working be relaxed, gentle, and unhurried for *effort defeats itself.*

"In quietness and in confidence shall be your strength" (Isa. 30:15).

THE LAW OF
SUBCONSCIOUS ACTIVITY

As soon as the subconscious mind accepts any idea, it immediately begins trying to put it into effect. It uses all its resources (and these are far greater than is commonly supposed) to that end. It uses every bit of knowledge that you have ever collected, and most of which you have totally forgotten, to bring about its purpose. It mobilizes the many mental powers that you possess and most of which you never consciously use. It draws on the unlimited energy of the race mind. It lines up all the laws of nature as they operate both inside and outside of you, to get its way.

Sometimes it succeeds in its purpose immediately. Sometimes it takes a little time; sometimes it takes a long time, depending on the difficulties to be overcome or the aspiration involved; but if the thing is not utterly impossible, the subconscious will bring it about—*once it accepts the idea.*

This law is true for both good and bad ideas. This law, when used negatively, brings sickness, trouble, and failure; and when used constructively, brings healing, freedom, and success. The Bible teaching does not say that harmony is inevitable no matter what we do—that is Pollyanna; it teaches that harmony is inevitable when our thoughts are positive, constructive, and kindly.

From this it follows that the only thing we have to do is to get the subconscious to accept the idea that we want reproduced, and the laws of nature will do the rest; will bring forth the healthy body, the harmonious circumstances, the successful career. We give the orders—the subconscious does the work.

As previously indicated this is essentially what spiritual treatment does. It gives a blueprint to the subconscious for it to work on. As we make our daily prayers and treatments, the subconscious accepts the idea, or ideas, and brings them into manifestation.

THE LAW OF PRACTICE

Practice makes perfect. This familiar proverb embodies one of the great laws of human nature. To become proficient in any field you must practice. There is simply no achievement without practice, and the more practice, provided it is done intelligently, the greater will be the proficiency and the sooner will it be attained. This is true in the study of music, in the study of a foreign language, in learning to swim or skate or ski or fly. It is true in every conceivable branch of human endeavor. *Practice is the price of proficiency.*

In business life and in any kind of management or administration, *experience* is the form that practice takes, and here again it is practice that makes perfect. That is why, other things being equal, an older person is usually to be selected for responsible positions rather than a younger.

In metaphysics the effects of this law are particularly striking. Thought control is entirely a matter of intelligent practice. And true religion may well be summed up as the Practice of the Presence of God. But note that I said *intelligent practice*. Violent forcing is not intelligent practice, nor is monotonous plodding.

Practice is the secret of attainment. We might paraphrase Danton and say practice! . . . and more practice!! . . . and still more practice!!!

"Be ye doers of the word, and not hearers only" (Jas. 1:22).

THE TWO FACTORS

Every thought is made up of two factors, knowledge and feeling. A thought consists of a piece of knowledge with a charge of feeling, and it is the feeling alone that gives power to the thought. No matter how important or magnificent the knowledge content may be, if there is no feeling attached to it nothing will happen. On the other hand, no matter how unimportant or insignificant the knowledge content may be, if there is a large charge of feeling something will happen.

This universal law is symbolized in nature by the bird. A bird has two wings, neither more nor less, and they must both be functioning before he can fly.

It makes no difference whether the knowledge content is correct or not as long as you *believe* it to be correct. Remember that it is what we really believe that matters. A report about something may be quite untrue, but if you believe it, it has the same effect upon you as if it were true; and that effect again will depend upon the quantity of feeling attached to it.

When we understand this Law we see the importance of accepting only the Truth concerning life in every phase of our experience. Indeed, this is why Jesus said, "Know the Truth and the Truth shall make you free" (John 8:32). Now we realize why negative feelings (fear, criticism, etc.) are so destructive, and a sense of peace and good will is such a power for healing.

WHAT YOU THINK
UPON GROWS

What you think upon grows. This is an Eastern maxim, and it sums up neatly the greatest and most fundamental of all the Laws of Mind. What you think upon grows.

What you think upon grows. Whatever you allow to occupy your mind you magnify in your own life. Whether the subject of your thought be good or bad, the law works and the condition grows. Any subject that you keep out of your mind tends to diminish in your life, because what you do not use atrophies.

The more you think about your indigestion or your rheumatism, the worse it will become. The more you think of yourself as healthy and well, the better will your body be.

The more you think about lack, bad times, et cetera, the

worse will be your business; and the more you think of prosperity, abundance, and success, the more of these things will you bring into your life.

The more you think about your grievances or the injustices that you have suffered, the more such trials will you continue to receive; and the more you think of the good fortune you have had, the more good fortune will come to you.

This is the basic, fundamental, all-inclusive Law of Mind, and actually all psychological and metaphysical teaching is little more than a commentary upon this.

*What you think upon grows.**

THE LAW OF FORGIVENESS

It is an unbreakable mental law that you have to forgive others if you want to demonstrate over your difficulties and to make any real spiritual progress.

The vital importance of forgiveness may not be obvious at first sight, but you may be sure that it is not by mere chance that every great spiritual teacher from Jesus Christ downward has insisted so strongly upon it.

You must forgive injuries, not just in words, or as a matter of form; but sincerely, in your heart—and that is the long and the short of it. You do this, not for the other person's sake, but for your own sake. It will make no difference to him (unless he happens to set a value upon your forgiveness), but it will make a tremendous difference to you. Resentment, condemnation, anger, desire to see someone punished are things that rot your soul, no matter how cleverly you may be disguising them. Such things, because they have a much stronger emotional con-

*See Philip. 4:8.

tent than anyone suspects, fasten your troubles to you with rivets. They fetter you to many other problems which actually have nothing whatever to do with the original grievances themselves.

Forgiveness does not mean that you have to like the delinquent or want to meet him; but that you must wish him well. Of course you must not make a "door mat" of yourself. You must not allow yourself to be imposed upon, or ill treated. You must fight your own battles and fight them with prayer, justice, and good will. It does not matter whether you can forget the injury or not, although if you cease to rehearse it you probably will—but you *must forgive*.

Now consider The Lord's Prayer.*

---

* This will be found as a chapter in *The Sermon on the Mount* and in *Power Through Constructive Thinking*.

Wealth

Emmet Fox was keenly aware that in the give-and-take of modern life, money is a vitally necessary ingredient. Yet he often said that a person who just piles up money merely has ink marks in a bankbook or pretty engravings on a stock certificate. These are all part of the modern economic system, but true wealth lies in what one has gained in consciousness. A man or woman can have great monetary wealth and be poor in everything else. It is the love *of money which is the root of evil, and in like proportion the* use *of money is its virtue.*

Emmet Fox points out that while the Bible teaches true prosperity and how to get it, nowhere does it guarantee to make anyone rich. He deals with the subject via an explanation of the oft-quoted statement of Jesus: "For unto every one that hath shall be given, and he shall have abundance: but from him that hath not shall be taken away even that which he hath" (Matt. 25:29). This is the text that has been twisted by scoffing unbelievers to read "The rich get richer and the poor get poorer."

This great text has been a stumbling block to many. It looks like injustice. It sounds like cruelty. Yet Jesus said it, and we know that he was always right; and that he taught that we reap as we sow.

The explanation is perfectly simple and logical when you have the metaphysical key to life. Your experience is the outpicturing or expression (pressing out) of your state of mind or consciousness, at any time. When your consciousness is high or relatively good, everything goes well. When your consciousness is relatively low or limited, everything goes wrong.

Trouble comes because the consciousness has fallen a little. The usual thing then is to meet the trouble with fear, anger, disappointment, self-pity, or brutal will power. This naturally lowers the consciousness a good deal more, and things get still worse—and so on. From him that hath not (much) harmony, shall be taken away even that which he hath.

Harmony and joy come into your life because your mental state is comparatively high. This happiness naturally raises your consciousness and your faith in God still higher, and so things improve further. Unto everyone that hath shall be given and he shall have abundance.

It applies to every department in life. The truth is that you can do anything, have anything, be anything, for which you have the consciousness—but not otherwise.

To be healthy, you must have a health consciousness. To be prosperous, you must have a prosperity consciousness. To be successful in any field of endeavor, you must have the consciousness that corresponds. There is a slang expression which says that to accomplish anything difficult "you must have what it takes." Well, what it "takes" is the consciousness to correspond with it.

The late Mike Todd typifies this. He made and lost several fortunes in his lifetime. At one of these low points a reporter asked, "Mike, how does it feel to be poor?"

Mike shot back, "I've never been poor. I have been broke but that's only a temporary thing. Poverty is a state of mind."

So in Jesus' statement, "To him that hath [in consciousness] shall be given," what seemed at first to be unjust and cruel turns out to be a trumpet call of courage and hope.

Having laid down the ground rules for acquiring abundance, Emmet Fox gets down to some practical cases.

True salesmanship consists in helping the "prospect" to obtain the merchandise that he really needs. This point must be stressed. It means *helping* the prospect. It means *service*. It does not mean taking advantage of him in any way. It certainly does not mean forcing upon him things that he does not need and cannot afford. Nor does it mean pretending to give him one article when in fact he is getting another and inferior one. Such a policy is no salesmanship at all. It is, in plain English, robbery.

True salesmanship means finding out what your customer really needs, and supplying him with it; or if you cannot furnish it yourself, advising him to go elsewhere. Such a policy will not, as many would suppose, mean loss of business. On the contrary, this method—merely the application of the Golden Rule—will build up your business more rapidly than anything else could. People sense honesty and sincerity intuitively, and these things beget confidence. Working in this way you may lose one order through your honesty, but you will get half a dozen in its place—and you will have peace of mind. Every intelligent salesman should know that any particular sale, or even any particular customer, does not matter, that it is the annual turnover that counts.

Certain courses of salesmanship used to say, "Get his name on the dotted line before you let him go." You should do the exact contrary to this. If there is any doubt in your own mind, or in his, tell him to think it over and come back later. If he does sign on the dotted line, and afterward you have any reason to suppose that he is not entirely satisfied, you should offer to release him immediately, and tear up the contract.

This policy, the Golden Rule, was taught by Jesus, the wisest and most practical teacher who ever lived; and *it is the secret of success in business*. It is the real key to sales promotion.

Salesman! Treat your customer exactly as you would like him to treat you if the positions were reversed. Tell him exactly what you would like to be told about the merchandise, if you were the purchaser; and if you will do this the whole universe will cooperate to make your business career an outstanding success.

Another case comes to mind. A man came to see me in London in great distress. He had attended some lectures I gave, and wanted advice.

He was the owner of a general grocery store in a village in the south of England, and hitherto there had been no competition. Now, one of the big chain stores was opening a branch almost opposite to him in the main street, and he was in a panic.

His father and grandfather had had the business before him, and he had spent his life in that one shop, living upstairs over it, and knew nothing else. He said, "How can I compete with them? I am ruined."

I said, "You have been studying the Truth for several years and you know the Great Law. You know where your supply comes from. Why be afraid?"

He said, "I must do something."

I said, "Stand in your shop each morning and bless it, by claiming that Divine Power works through it for great prosperity and peace for all concerned." He nodded his head in agreement.

I added, "Then step out on the sidewalk, look down the street to where they are fitting up the new store, and bless that in the same way."

"What? Cut my own throat?" he almost screamed. "Am I to help them against myself?"

I explained that what blesses one, blesses all; that treatment is creative and makes more business—more prosperity —and that the only thing that could impoverish him was his own fear. I told him that he was really hating his competitor (through fear) and that his hatred could destroy him, and that blessing the "enemy" was the way to get rid of hate. I finished by saying, "You cannot cut your throat with prayer; you can only improve everything."

It took some time to persuade him, but at last he got the idea and carried it out; and when I met him several years later he told me that *his business had been better than ever* since the chain store appeared; and that they seemed to be getting on well too. He was prosperous and had peace.

This is what Jesus meant when he said, "Love your enemies."

A large proportion of what are called business problems really consist in negotiating with other people. All sales-manship as we have seen is negotiation between the seller and the purchaser. And successful salesmanship means bringing that negotiation to a termination satisfactory to *both* parties.

Whether you are seeking a position for yourself or engaging someone else to work for you, the ultimate outcome will depend on negotiation. You want to find the right person to fill your vacancy or you wish to be engaged for a certain position that you think would suit your requirements very well, and in either case the outcome is a matter of negotiation. Disputes and misunderstandings often arise between two business firms or between a firm and a customer, and here again harmonious relations in the future— which means more business—will depend upon how the present negotiations are conducted.

In fact, every relation in life will be found to depend upon the ability to make harmonious personal adjustments, which is negotiation. In such matters as family and personal disputes, as well as in those things more usually considered under the head of business, the same principle will be found to apply with even greater force if possible.

Now, the secret of successful negotiation can be put into a nutshell. It is this: *See God on both sides of the table.* Claim that God is working through both of you, through yourself and through the person with whom you are dealing. Do not seek by will power to get your own way, but affirm that God's will in that particular matter is being done. Remember that your own way may not be at all good for you. The very thing that you want today may turn out next week to be a nuisance or even a misfortune. Do not try to overreach the other man, to persuade him against his will, or to take the slightest advantage of him in any way. But state your case honestly to the best of your ability; do only what you think is right; and know that God is living and working in your life. Then if you do not get that job, or hire that person, you will get a better one. If you do not make the arrangement that you sought today, a better one will present itself tomorrow.

Never allow yourself to be strained or tense or over-eager. God never hurries; He works without effort. In dealing with fellow man *put God on both sides of the table*, and the outcome will be true success for both parties.

And then as Emmet Fox does with so many of his golden keys, he takes you a step further and says, "Capitalize your disability"—if you think you have one.

Success consists in overcoming of difficulties. All men and women who have made a success of any kind have done so by overcoming difficulties. Where there are no difficulties to be overcome, anybody can get the thing done, and doing so cannot be called success—it is routine.

There was a time when laying a telegraph line from New York to Boston presented many difficulties. Then there was a time when doing that was easy but laying the Atlantic cable was a great achievement, because of the difficulties which had to be overcome. Then came radio, television, and all the other electronic marvels. Each step presented new challenges which were overcome.

There are no personal problems that cannot be overcome by quiet, persistent spiritual treatment, and the appropriate wise activity.

If you have a personal disability that seems to keep you from success, do not accept it as such, but *capitalize it* and use it as the instrument for your success.

H. G. Wells had to give up a dull underpaid job because of ill health, so he stayed at home and wrote successful books and became a world-known author instead. Edison was stone deaf and decided that this would enable him to concentrate better on his inventions. Beethoven did his work in spite of his deafness. Theodore Roosevelt was a sickly child and was told he would have to lead a careful retired life. He was a very shortsighted and nervous little boy. Instead of accepting these suggestions, however, he worked hard to develop his body and became, as we know, a strong, husky, open-air man and big game hunter. Gilbert wrote Pinafore on a sick bed, wracked with severe pain.

The owner of a fashionable dress business in London was the wife of a struggling clerk. He was stricken with tuberculosis. She had never been to business and had no training of any kind, and found herself having to support a husband and two children. She started with nothing but good taste in clothes and a belief in prayer, and became a wealthy and successful woman. She said, "I thought I would like to sell the kind of clothes I had never been able to afford to buy."

Whatever you think your disability is—*capitalize it*. Your particular problem will always seem to be especially difficult, but spiritual treatment and courageous determination can overcome anything.

Problems are the signpost on the road to God.

The
Moron
Club

At first glance one would hardly think that being a member of the Moron Club would be a golden key to successful living, but with Emmet Fox's inimitable sense of humor it becomes exactly that. He holds up the mirror of satire so we can have a good look.

MR. ATLAS

It is proverbial that the troubles which worry us most are the ones we never have to meet. Countless people have been killed by misfortunes that never happened to them. This looks absurd on paper but it is tragically true in life. Of all the types of foolish people, Mr. Atlas probably takes the palm. Not satisfied with his own many troubles (and Mr. Atlas is certain to have a great many of his very own), he has to go about worrying over everybody else's problem too. The Greeks pictured him carrying the whole world on his own shoulders, bowed down under the intolerable weight, and this is a splendid symbol of what many people are doing today.

Mind your own business, Mr. Atlas. Hoe your own row, scrub your own doorstep, and that will give you quite enough to do—if you do it properly. Do not try to carry the burdens of the whole world. Such a policy will destroy you and will not help the world.

Leave something to God. After all, it is He who is responsible for the world, and not you. Has it ever occurred to you that if *you* had never been born, the world would have had to get along somehow, and that God would probably take care of everything quite well?

To worry over conditions that you cannot change is gratuitous folly. To get and to keep your own peace of mind, to do your own duties well, and to see the Presence of God in all men and things, is the surest way both to help the world, and to make your own life divinely successful too.

Drop that globe, Mr. Atlas, and straighten up, and look at the sky.

MRS. FIX-IT

She is probably the most energetic member in the Club, and is well in the running for the Presidency. Everyone knows her, and few indeed have managed to escape her attentions. She is indefatigable, inescapable, unsnubbable. Nothing discourages her; to mere hints she is impervious—she means so well. She doesn't interfere in cold blood, it is simply an instinct with her—*she must try to fix it*. She has been interfering from the moment of her birth, trying to put everything right, and, needless to say, usually making things worse, doing more harm than good in the long run.

She has a passion for putting the other fellow's house in order. In a very literal sense, I have known her when she was a guest in a house, actually to proceed to rearrange the furniture and the pictures, telling her hostess where she was wrong.

Of course, she manages her entire family. Her brothers

and her sisters and her cousins and her aunts have to toe the line—*her line*. She prescribes their diet, tells them when they can afford a car and which model to buy; or puts her foot down and says that for the present they ought to walk. The education of their children is a constant preoccupation with her, and she often tries to censor their friendships too. God help her parents, for, as a rule, no human power can save them. Her colleagues, if she is in business, and her associates elsewhere dread her approach, and flee if there is yet time.

Mrs. Fix-it has her good points of course. She is apt to be as generous with her money as with her advice. She is nearly always disinterested, wanting nothing for herself, sincerely desirous only of helping others. Her basic error is love gone wrong, as love is so apt to when not balanced by intelligence. Give Mrs. Fix-it the right thought, but for heaven's sake keep at a safe distance from her.

SWEET ALICE (BEN BOLT)

She is no longer an actual member but there is a beautiful plaque to her memory in the lobby of the Club. It is felt that her untimely demise robbed the Club of one of its most promising recruits. You remember her peculiarity, of course. She was afraid of everyone:

> She wept with delight when you gave her a smile,
> And trembled with fear at your frown.

Nothing mattered to her except other people's opinion. Not what she was, but what other people thought about her, was the important thing.

Modern medical science would have called this a case of acute neurasthenia, and prescribed special diet, open air exercise, et cetera; but our grandparents were merely sen-

timental about it. After this we are not in the least surprised to hear that

> She lies under a stone.

Nothing else could be expected. Nor does it help a bit that
the stone is

> In an old church-yard in the valley.

though this was evidently thought to be important.

The fact that a beautiful air is attached to these foolish
verses only shows how a false sentiment will try to conceal
itself behind something good.

Do not be a slave to other people's opinion. Do what
you know is right, and care for no man's censure. *Serve
God and fear no one.* It does not matter in the least
whether you please other people; it matters that you are
loyal to God and to your own soul. As a matter of fact,
those who are always trying to please everyone, seldom
succeed in pleasing anyone. They tear their emotional na-
tures to pieces instead of building serenity and poise.

With God on your side you can fearlessly look the world
in the face.

SEE-SAW SIMPSON

In a popular novel of the last generation, there was a
boy whom his comrades nicknamed See-Saw Simpson, because he was constantly changing his mind. He is now a
middle-aged man and has been a prominent member of
the Club for many years, in fact, he is Second Vice-Presi-
dent.

Brother Simpson never knows his own mind for twenty-
four hours at a time. He is usually of the opinion of the

last person who has talked to him, but not infrequently he switches again as soon as he is alone once more. His drifting mentality simply cannot crystallize in any direction. In the words of the Bible, he is cursed with the curse of Reuben—*unstable as water, thou shalt not excel.* He is sincere, good-natured, and well-meaning, but his character is so weak that he cannot take a definite attitude on any point and hold to it. He has no definite principles. He does not know where he stands on any subject, nor does anyone else.

The natural consequence of all this, of course, is that in business he has been a drifting failure, and that in all social relationships he is sure to be the one who is overlooked. No one trusts Brother Simpson because no one ever knows what he will do next. It is impossible to make satisfactory arrangements with him about anything, because the next time you see him he will have changed his mind and let you down. And very likely he will soon afterward change it back again.

Make up your mind. Do one thing or the other, but in Heaven's name do not see-saw about indefinitely. If you take a decisive step, you may be wrong; but if you see-saw, you are certain to be wrong.

If indecisiveness is your failing, practice making snap decisions in the following way: When the occasion arises say, *the Christ is guiding me*; and then do one thing or the other *quickly*. Then stick to your choice, in spite of any doubts you may have to the contrary. If you really believe what you have said, that the Christ is guiding you, your decision must be the right one. Keep this practice up for some weeks and, while you will make mistakes in the beginning, you will rapidly find yourself making quick and almost effortless decisions which turn out to be correct, and this will become a habit.

WILBUR WEAKFISH

He is easily the most popular member of the Club. Everyone likes him. He is so kind. Indeed, his kindness is a byword among his friends, and most of them say he is the nicest man they ever met, a real good sport with a heart as big as his body.

He is indeed very kind to *almost* everyone—and in that "almost" lies the tragedy, for it gives the other side of the story.

Wilbur Weakfish is always popular with strangers because he cannot say *no* to them. It is only those who are nearest to him who ever hear that word. He is so full of philanthropy that there is no room in him for the word *duty*. He gives money to strangers because he cannot say *no*, although his wife needs a winter coat. He presents the Club with a new set of bookcases for the library, for which he receives an illuminated address of thanks from the President, handed to him at a full meeting—but the landlord does not get his rent for a couple of months and the family is humiliated and threatened with dispossession.

He likes to see his name high up on every subscription list, but a large sum of money which he borrowed from his brother nearly ten years ago has never been repaid; and when his eldest boy was ready to enter college there was no money for him, and he had to find a job instead.

Why does he do it? People say it is because he is kind-hearted. Nothing of the sort. It is because he is selfish and weak. He loves to be thanked effusively, to play Lord Bountiful; and one does not get this for doing one's duty. He cannot say *no* because he does not want to. He prefers to enjoy himself at anyone's expense.

CALAMITY JANE

She is the most regular attendant at Club meetings, but
even there she cannot be said to be popular, and everywhere else she is disliked. She is almost a hereditary member because her uncle, Dismal Daniel, was one of the
founders of the Club, although he said at the time that he
did not think it could succeed. He underestimated the
potential membership.

Calamity Jane is a chronic pessimist. She sees the dark
side of everything immediately, and nothing else. She always anticipates the worst. When anything new is started,
she says it cannot succeed, or that it is now too late. And
when things are obviously going well, she shakes her head
mournfully and says they are too good to last. Her role in
life seems to be to discourage, as far as she can, everyone
she comes across; and she is usually fairly successful in this.
She is a born wet blanket; joy cannot live in her presence.
No matter how enthusiastic people may be, Jane's arrival
lowers the temperature toward zero.

According to Jane, the country is shot to pieces and cannot recover. The state in which she lives has no future
because the climate is bad and the soil is exhausted; and
her city, she says, is doomed, because it is badly situated
anyway, and those who govern it are a bunch of crooks.

Of course her own life is beset with constant difficulties.
Her health is poor. She grumbles ceaselessly about her
whole digestive tract, which is naturally in a bad way, and
causes her daily torment; and she says there is no hope for
it, because it runs in the family and that her uncle Daniel
had just the same trouble. Her financial and business affairs are so involved that they make her life a constant
misery. She never knows where next month's rent is coming from, and sometimes this applies to last month's rent as

well. Of course she can no more have prosperity than she can have health, with the mental model she has built for herself. But she seems incapable of realizing this, and goes on destroying her own health, happiness, and prosperity day after day. She is the only enemy that she has in the world.

When Emmet Fox first wrote about these members of the Moron Club, he chided the reader into giving a second thought to each one by appending a postscript to each Member: "Does Calamity Jane (etc.) remind you at all of someone whose name you often sign?"

I should point out that when Emmet Fox said such things as these from the platform, he would often add, "Now, I'm not talking to you; I'm talking to the person next to you!" And everyone would laugh! Then he would say, "Now, that's better. I think everyone was getting a little tense." He would then carry on, with the audience in an open, receptive mood.

The reason he sometimes chose this "negative" approach to teaching the Truth was that he realized the negative often has much greater impact than the positive. For example, newspaper reporting, as he often mentioned, is largely built on the negative approach.

It is news when it is rumored that a princess or a film star is getting a divorce. Readers are anxious to know more. But report that someone has been happily married for twenty-three years, and the response is "So what."

Jesus used the "negative" approach at least once to get across the message of the power of thought. He and his disciples were walking along the dusty road toward the city, and the Bible notes that they were hungry (Matt. 21:18). Coming upon a fig tree with no figs on it, Jesus spoke to the tree: "Let no fruit grow on thee henceforward forever." And presently the fig tree withered away. It was a dramatic demonstration of the power of thought used negatively.

Jesus could just as easily have produced figs on the tree, which would have been his normal procedure. In that case the disciples would have eaten their fill and said, "Oh, leave it to the Master; he always demonstrates"—and gone their way. But to come along hungry and have the prize snatched right out of their mouths was a lesson they would not soon forget. They probably pondered this "negative" demonstration for a long time and finally realized, to some extent at least, the tremendous potential resident in each for either good or evil.

Why not take another look at the Moron Club. Perhaps one of the members has something to suggest to you that would be your golden key.

Reincarnation
and Life
After Death

In these golden keys of knowledge Emmet Fox has added considerably to the understanding of life. And I have often been asked how he acquired so much knowledge. Well, I think that his discourse on Reincarnation gives at least part of the answer, and I would add to that—pure inspiration. Inspiration gives anyone who seeks it in any particular field to which he gives his attention, knowledge and information that no one else has. For example, look at the work of a great composer. Where do his themes and original melodies come from? There is only one source: Divine Mind. So it was with Emmet Fox. The greater part of his lifetime was devoted to the search for facets of Truth, and that could only culminate in unveiling to mankind some of these mysteries.

Reincarnation is not taught in the Bible but is referred to obliquely. For example, when Jesus asked his disciples, "Whom do men say that I the Son of man am?" They answered, "Some say that thou art John the Baptist: some, Elias; and others, Jeremias, or one of the prophets." And then Jesus said unto

*them, "But whom say ye that I am?" And Peter in a
flash of pure inspiration, understanding the mystical
nature of Reincarnation, replied, "Thou art the
Christ, the Son of the living God." And Jesus answered and said unto him, "Blessed art thou, Simon
Bar-jo-na: for flesh and blood hath not revealed it
unto thee, but my Father which is in heaven," that
is, Divine revelation or inspiration. That is true of
each one of us. In essence each one reincarnates as
the son of the living God. (See Matt. 16:13–17.)*

*Now, Jesus could have been very explicit about
Reincarnation because he knew it answers questions
about life that are otherwise unanswerable, but he
was undoubtedly very familiar with the Eastern
teachings on Reincarnation with its postponement of
the solution of problems; with its easy attitude, "Why
concern myself with that now. I can work it out in
the next incarnation."*

*Jesus had an entirely different view. His idea was
"Now is the day of salvation; now is the accepted
time." And indeed this is the only way that progress
can be made in the world.*

*Emmet Fox has a good deal to say about Reincarna-
tion. He begins by asking some questions:*

Have you ever asked yourself why there should be such a
difference between one human lot and another? Have you
ever wondered why some people seem to be so happy and
fortunate in their lives, while others appear to undergo so
much undeserved suffering? Why should this be, if indeed
God is Love, and if God is just, and if God is all-powerful?

Well, the answer is that this life that you are living
today is not the only life; and that it cannot be understood
when judged by itself. The answer is that you have lived

before, not once, but many, many times, and that in the course of these many lives you have *thought and said and done* all sorts of things, good and bad, and that the circumstances into which you were born are but the natural outcome of the way in which you have lived and comported yourself in your former lives. You are reaping today, for good or evil, the results of the seeds that you have sown during these many previous lives. And in future ages, centuries from now very likely, you will return to this earth planet and be born again as a baby in some family; and grow up, and probably marry, and live out another life. And the conditions under which you start that life will be the outcome of the lives you have already lived; but most particularly will they be the outcome of the life which you are living at the present time. That, briefly, is the story of the life of man. What is customarily called a lifetime is really but a comparatively brief day in a long, long life.

You will not only come back, but you will probably meet some of your present associates again, particularly if there is an emotional link either of love or hatred between you. Love will take care of itself; but you must get all hatred out of your heart, if you do not want to renew disagreeable contacts.*

In the same way, some of your present associates are sure to be people with whom you had dealings in a previous life or lives. Your son today may have been your father, or merely an acquaintance in days gone by, and a close friend today may in other times have been a relative or a husband, or wife. The general tendency is for people who live and move in the same groups to reincarnate about the same time, although, of course, there will always be exceptions.

*See "The Lord's Prayer" in *Power Through Constructive Thinking,* or in *The Sermon on the Mount.*

Apropos of what Emmet Fox says here, two cases come to mind. One is of a lovely lady taking beautiful care of a semi-invalid husband, and very much in love with him, who told me she felt sure that she had killed him in a previous life, and the present situation was a natural Karma. Another case is that of a young woman recently married, who said she felt that she had been her husband's mother in a previous life. And when I asked her why, she said she did not know but that she simply had a deep feeling that that was the case.

Regardless of any question of Reincarnation, it must be remembered that this earth life can be a most interesting and joyous process in itself, for this is a wonderful world (of which even now man only knows about five percent) and your sojourn here can be a series of wonderful and joyous adventures, if only you will learn the laws of life and apply them. Progress is made by overcoming the practical difficulties of our everyday lives, not by running away from them. Jesus, knowing this, said that he would not pray that his followers should be taken out of the world, but rather that they should remain in the world and develop naturally there. And, indeed, that is just what the world is for.

Why is Reincarnation necessary? Why should life have to develop in that particular way? The reason is this: We are here to develop spiritually. We are here to acquire full understanding of and control over our mentality; and this cannot be done in one lifetime. The explanation lies in man's mental laziness and inertia; in his reluctance to change himself radically; to adopt new ideas and adapt himself to changing conditions. There are other reasons why the reincarnating of the ego many times is necessary.

Nature wants you to have all kinds of experience in order to develop every side of your character.* This is why Reincarnation is necessary. You will see now what a simple and natural process it is. The idea seems a strange and startling one at first only because we in the West have been totally unaware of it. But in the East it is as familiar a fact as the rising and setting of the sun, and it is probable that the majority of mankind have always believed in Reincarnation.

Why do you not remember your previous lives? Well, you do not remember the early days of this life. For various reasons Nature has drawn a veil of forgetfulness over our beginnings on this plane, and for excellent reasons she hides away the memory of previous lives until we are sufficiently developed to be ready to remember them. It would not be well for most people to be able to recollect their previous lives, because at the present time they simply could not stand it.

Meanwhile, some people do get an occasional glimpse of their past incarnations in one way or another, and, if wisely handled, such glimpses can be extremely useful. And there are those who get more than a glimpse. As a matter of fact, the whole history of all your past lives is stored away in the deeper levels of your subconscious, and thus it is that your mentality today—and consequently your destiny—is the logical outcome of all the lives that you have lived up to the present.

> Our deeds still travel with us from afar,
> And what we have been, makes us what we are.

We must consider the question of how the baby comes to be born in the particular family in which it is born; how

*See chapter "The Stars in Their Courses."

you, for example, came to be born into the particular family into which you were born. Let me begin by saying that the Stork never makes a mistake. Each one of us is born into the conditions which exactly fit his soul at the time of incarnation. He naturally gravitates to the exact spot that belongs to him.

Now we are ready to understand the startling statement that *there is no such thing as heredity*. This statement will surprise many, but it is true. No one ever "inherits" anything from his parents or his ancestors. He already had certain mental tendencies guide him to a family where similar tendencies existed—that is all. One does not "inherit" arthritis or weak kidneys from his father or his grandmother; he joins a family of that type because he already has these conditions potentially. Like attracts like all through the universe, or, as we say more picturesquely, *birds of a feather flock together.*

Reincarnation explains at once the differences in talents which we find between one man and another, just as it explains all the other differences. Why has one man a special aptitude for music, another for engineering, and yet a third for farming, while so many seem to have no particular aptitude at all? Differences in talent, like differences in opportunity, are the result of our activities in other lives. The born musician is a man who has studied music in a previous life, perhaps in several lives, and has therefore built that faculty into his soul. He is a talented musician today because he is reaping what he sowed yesterday. In like manner, child prodigies are always souls who have acquired their proficiency in a previous life.

An understanding of Reincarnation solves most of life's riddles and utterly changes the perspective of the whole thing. It is the sovereign remedy for depression and discouragement and regret. It is the gospel of freedom and hope. It makes us realize that there is no mistake that cannot be repaired, that it is never too late, and that no good thing is out of reach of intelligence and work and prayer. It shows us all a future in which there is no limit to the glorious things that we may be and do.

As you think over the truth of Reincarnation and gradually assimilate it—for an adequate realization of what this great truth really means is not to be obtained in a day or two—you will be astonished at the number of otherwise insoluble problems which it clears up. The major problems of life are logically and satisfactorily explained by Reincarnation, and all sorts of minor difficulties which have puzzled you from time to time fall easily into place too when the great scheme of things is understood.

I think the reader will see that included in Reincarnation is the Law of Cause and Effect. Jesus was very much aware of this for he says that you do not gather grapes from thorns or figs from thistles; and he also said, *"by their fruits ye shall know them."** So it is with our thoughts and words and deeds. As we sow, we reap. When we sow good, we reap good, and when we sow evil, we reap trouble and suffering. This is the great Law of Cause and Effect, yet it is amazing that people seem to understand it as little as they do.

In the East this Law of Cause and Effect is known as Karma and the term is a convenient one, but whatever we choose to call it, the law of nature still stands, that as we sow, we shall reap, whether the sowing was done in a previous lifetime or this one. However, no matter what mistakes you have made in the past or what opportunities you have wasted, you can overtake them all now; for your future stretches out to infinity and it is never too late with

*Read Matt. 7:15-20; Luke 6:43-45.

God. Cease the wrong conduct, make whatever reparation, if any, is possible, make your peace with God, and then turn your back on the past and never think about it again. Remember that to harbor useless regrets is remorse instead of repentance, and remorse is a sin.

Note very carefully that Karma is not punishment. You suffer because you have a lesson to learn, but when the lesson is learned, the ill consequences cease, for nature is never vindictive. It is unfortunate that some people talk so much about "bad Karma." You have seen now that no Karma is bad at all, and, further, such people are dwelling exclusively on the suffering that follows wrong conduct. It is just as much the Law of Karma that every good and kind and wise thing you have said or done has brought you fruit of its own kind and will continue to do so. Especially every moment in your life that you have spent in prayer or meditation will continue to bless and enrich you to the end of time. Here I wish to make it clear as I possibly can that there is nothing fatalistic about the Law of Karma. You have free will—not omnipotence—but always a choice within reasonable limits—and always you can choose the higher or the lower.

The Law of Karma teaches that by making the best use of whatever talents or advantages we have, even though they be small, we shall win still greater talents and opportunities. Jesus teaches this in Matthew 25:15–30. On the other hand, if we neglect to make the best use of our talents and opportunities, we shall lose even what we have. As the Bible says, God gave him that talent, that opportunity, and he "buries it in a napkin."

Most of the trouble in our lives is not caused by Karma at all but by lack of wisdom in the present. The conditions in which you began your life were karmic, but your everyday experience is made by yourself as you go along. It is a common failing for people to behave unwisely and then grumble at their difficulties and lay the blame on Karma.

I knew a student of this subject who constantly talked in this way. He was the proprietor of a small business which was steadily failing, and he was surrounded by debts and other embarrassments. He was full of self-pity and he would enlarge upon his worries, and say what a terrible sinner he must have been in his last life to be "punished" in this way. Now the fact was, as some of his friends well knew, that he had no idea of running a business properly. His shop looked neglected, and the quality of his goods was inferior to that obtainable elsewhere at the same price. He was constantly out of stock of the commonest things that customers would ask for, and he was continually borrowing money at high interest to overtake other debts. Obviously, all this had nothing to do with Karma. His Karma, as far as it went, was good, because it had given him a business of his own in which many men would have made a great success. His trouble was poor judgment and, to some extent, laziness. Two or three of his friends who realized these facts and grew tired of his complaints once made an effort to bring the truth home to him for his own good, but their efforts were not well received, and he could not or would not face the truth.

Finally, and perhaps this is the most important point of all, you do not have to accept any set of conditions or any kind of Karma if you will rise *above* it in consciousness. Any difficulty, any dilemma, can be surmounted by wholehearted prayer. A given difficulty can only confront you on its own level. Rise above that level through prayer and meditation and the difficulty will melt away. You do not, as so many people think, have to sit down and eat your Karma with as good grace as possible, if you can rise above that situation in consciousness. On its own level you have to accept it—you cannot transmute it there. But rise above any ordeal in consciousness and you will be free from it—for the Christ is Lord of Karma.*

> Our birth is but a sleep and a forgetting
>   The Soul that rises with us, our Life's Star,
>   Hath had elsewhere its setting,
>   And cometh from afar;
>   Not in entire forgetfulness,
>   And not in utter nakedness,
>   But trailing clouds of glory do we come
>   From God, who is our home.

—Wordsworth

Now, having gotten us established in this life, what about the next life. Emmet Fox has answered many questions concerning that too. He says:

There is absolutely no reason to fear death. The same God is on the other side of the grave as on this side, and the Bible tells us that God is Love, and we know that He is also boundless Intelligence and Infinite Power. It is true that most people do fear death more or less, but this fear is partly that normal fear of the unknown that is apt to affect us all—the fear, as it were, of taking a leap in the dark—and partly it is the result of the false teaching on the subject that most people acquire in their youth.

The actual truth is that there is no death. When a person seems to die, all that happens is that he leaves his body here and goes over onto the next plane, otherwise un-

*See *The Sermon on the Mount*, chap. 6.

changed. He falls asleep here to wake up on the other side minus his physical body (which was probably more or less damaged) but enriched with the knowledge that he has not really died.

This is the story of what we call "death," and in most cases it is easier than being born.

To understand clearly how this process comes about, you have to realize that you really possess not one body but two. It may surprise you to be told that right here at the present moment you have not only the physical body that you know about—the thing that you see when you look into the glass—but a second body—the etheric body. It is the same shape as your physical body, but it is slightly larger and it interpenetrates the physical body as air fills a sponge. There are a few people who can see the etheric body when they concentrate for that purpose because they have the power of contacting much finer vibrations than can be perceived by the ordinary physical senses.

All the time you are awake, your two bodies remain together interpenetrating each other, but when you fall asleep, the greater part of your etheric slips out of the physical; and in reality this slipping out of the etheric is what constitutes sleep. The same sort of thing happens when you become unconscious either from taking an anesthetic or from a blow on the head, or if you fall into what is called a trance, or into some form of coma. All these conditions differ somewhat one from another, but they all have this in common, that more or less of the etheric slips out of the physical body taking consciousness with it.

It is this etheric body which is the repository of all your thoughts and feelings. It includes what are often called the conscious and subconscious minds. It is the "psyche" of the psychologist, and it is in fact your *human personality*. That is why personality survives death, because it resides in the etheric which passes over intact, and not in the physical which breaks up into decomposition when it is left alone.

I have said that your etheric is the seat of all feeling, and this is true. It may surprise you to hear that there is no sensation in the physical body, but such is the case. When you think you have a pain in your physical body, that pain is really in the etheric counterpart, and that is why anesthesia is possible. When you take a general anesthetic, the etheric is thrown out and therefore you do not experience bodily sensations. People undergoing a major operation under an anesthetic have sometimes remained perfectly conscious, but out of the body, and have watched the surgeon at work with interest and attention. When you take a local anesthetic such as novocaine, the local part of the etheric is driven out and you have no feeling there; but as the effect of the novocaine wears off, that portion of the etheric returns and, as those who have been in the hands of the dentist know, the pain gradually comes back.

In all these cases when the etheric leaves the physical body, it remains attached to it by an etheric ligament very much like a boy's kite floating at the end of the string which he holds in his hand. This etheric connection is called in the Bible the Silver Cord. It is bluish gray in color and is so elastic that the etheric body can go very long distances away and still remain attached to the physical corpus. In sleep, by far the greater part of the etheric slips out. The difference between normal sleep, anesthesia, and the different kinds of trance* is a question of how much of the etheric goes out at that particular time. So your etheric slips out every time you go to sleep and returns when you wake up again—that is, as long as the Silver Cord remains *unbroken*.

*Num. 24:4; Acts 10:10, 11:5, 22:17.

Death is the breaking of the Silver Cord. As long as that remains intact you are alive, whether you are conscious or not; but once it is broken you are dead. You are definitely cut off from your physical body and your life on this plane is over.

What precisely is it that happens to a person when he dies—when the Silver Cord is severed? What does he think? What does he feel? Well, as a rule, he immediately falls into a state of total unconsciousness which may last for days or even weeks. During this time the etheric (that is he himself) passes over onto the next plane, and he is in the next world. Here in due course he wakes up very much as we wake up from sleep on this plane, and his new life has begun.

It is an interesting fact that at the instant preceding death, the whole of the past life unfolds before the mind exactly like a moving picture reel flashing by. The actual speed is so great that it all happens in a split second. Yet the mind sees every detail clearly. It is possible to come so near death that without actually dying one can still come back and continue to live after this has happened, but usually only in cases of near-death from asphyxiation. Only in near-drowning, suffocation, or gassing, as a rule, is the process slow enough to admit of this. This experience is really the unfolding of the subconscious mind, the "Judgment Books" of Scripture, and an exceedingly awe-inspiring and sometimes terrible experience it is, as one can easily imagine. It is with this authentic inside story of his life fresh in his memory that the traveler begins his life on the other side.

I am very familiar with an example of what Emmet Fox records here. When my father was a youth, he was sail-boating on the Shrewesbury River in New Jersey when a sudden gust of wind came up and over-

turned the boat. In the accident he was knocked un-
conscious by the swinging boom and dumped into
the water. He was rescued by other boaters, but in his
unconscious state he was nearly drowned, and later
he remembered very clearly that his whole life had
flashed through his mind and the whole experience
was a terrifying one.

It sometimes happens when a person "dies" that instead
of his going into a coma immediately after the Silver Cord
is broken, there may be an interval of hours or longer in
which he retains full possession of his faculties; and sometimes he does not even realize that he is "dead," though as
a rule he sees his physical body lying prone and knows
what has happened. In such cases he will make a strong
effort to communicate with his closest friends. Suppose, for
example, that a man died in the street and retained his
faculties in this way. He would immediately try to get
home to his wife to tell her what had happened. Let us
suppose that his home was ten miles away in the suburbs.
Having now only an etheric body, he would really need
but to think strongly of his home and he would find himself there in a few seconds or less, because his etheric body
could pass through houses, hills, or any other physical obstruction that might lie in the way. However, habit might
lead him to go through the motions of walking to the
nearest railroad station and getting into a train, or he
might clamber into a bus. On entering his home he would
instinctively shout to his wife, but having no physical or-
gans, no sound would be produced and she would hear
nothing. Or he might attempt to grasp her arm, but his
etheric substance would simply pass through it without
making any impression. It might happen, however, in such
a case that the strong mental effort would reach the con-

sciousness of the wife and then afterward she would say, "My husband appeared to me for a moment at the time he was killed." His thought would be so charged with emotion that it would be strong enough, upon reaching her, to cause her to project a momentary thought form of him. Or she might say, "I knew that something had happened to my husband long before I got the news." This is the explanation of most such stories which are so constantly met with.

In the same way, people have sometimes attended their own funerals.

At this point it is natural to ask: Where is the next world situated? The next world is actually all around us here. The so-called dead are carrying on their lives right here where we are now, but in their own world and in their own way. The reason we do not see them around us or collide with them is the same reason that one television program does not interfere with another—they are on different wave lengths.

What is it that determines the kind of place to which you will go after death? No one "sends" you anywhere. You naturally gravitate to the place where you belong. You have built up a certain mentality by your years of thinking, speaking, and acting on this plane. That is the kind of person you are at the moment, and you find yourself in conditions corresponding to your personality. On this earth, people with the same interests tend to attract one another. The law that "birds of a feather flock together" holds throughout the universe.

You do not "meet God" on the next plane any more than you do on this plane. God is everywhere. He is fully present on the next plane just as He is on this plane. There as here, He is to be contacted only in one's own consciousness by some form of prayer or spiritual treatment. On the other hand, Heaven is that perfect state of consciousness in which one is in full realization of the Divine Presence. In that consciousness there is no limitation, or evil, or decay of any kind. When one attains to that condition he has finished with etheric planes just as surely as he has finished with the plane of physical matter. If you can reach to that level of consciousness while still in this world (and a few have succeeded in doing so) you do not "die" or go across to the etheric planes at all; you go straight to Heaven from this earth. Moses did this, and Enoch, and Elijah, and a few others. This is what is called translation or dematerialization. It is accomplished by the overcoming of the sense of separation from God which is really the "fall of man." It means overcoming selfishness, sensuality, criticism, fear, and other such things. It means living near and nearer to God every day. Of Enoch,* the Bible says "he walked with God" before he was translated —and indeed there is no other way to freedom.

Will you meet your relatives and friends when you go over? People naturally wonder whether they will see again those whom they loved who have passed out of sight; and some are quite apprehensive of having to renew their contact with people whom they have disliked—members of the family perhaps whom they would much prefer never to meet again. The fact is that where there is a strong emotional link either of love or hatred there is likely to be a meeting. Where there is a strong link of genuine love there is sure to be a meeting. Where there is no particular feeling between two people there will not be a meeting.

Of course, love will take care of itself, but there is a real danger that if you allow yourself to indulge in hatred of anyone, you will meet when you have both passed over. To

* Gen. 5:24.

prevent this from happening, destroy the link by ceasing to hate. Forgive the other person and set him free in your thought, and you will have set yourself free too. You do not have to like him but you must wish him well.*

Do not imagine that your family will ever be reassembled on the other side. Family relationships are for this plane only and have no existence there.

Of course, it seems very hard to tell people not to grieve when one whom they have dearly loved passes out of sight; but the fact remains that excessive grief is bad for both parties. Remember that if there is a link of love you will certainly meet again, and that nothing that is good or beautiful or true can ever be lost.

We can pray for those who have passed on, and indeed it is a sacred duty to do so. Prayers for the so-called dead have been used in most parts of the world in most ages. The practice was generally discontinued after the Reformation because it had been greatly abused and commercialized, but nevertheless, it is an excellent practice in itself. You should pray for your friend who has passed on exactly as you would pray for him if he were living in some distant spot on this globe. Realize peace of mind, freedom, and understanding for him, and that God is Life and Intelligence and Love. *The Presence*** is excellent for this purpose. Read it to him silently, saying "You" where the text says "I."

You should realize this fact very clearly: There is nothing whatever sacred about a dead body. It is a collection of physical matter for which the ex-owner has no further use. Its late owner wore out a number of physical bodies during his life (as you probably know, we get a number of

*See "The Lord's Prayer" in *Power Through Constructive Thinking*.
** In *Power Through Constructive Thinking*.

new bodies by gradual replacement as we go through life) and this is only the last of them. Remember that the beauty of a beautiful body comes from the soul that shines through it and does not lie in the body itself. That soul with its beauty and joy has now gone on, and the body left is but an old garment which has been discarded. This garment should be disposed of (for the sake of the living) with respect, but not with reverence; and the proper method of doing this is by cremation. The body having been cremated, it is better not to preserve the ashes. They should be disposed of with a prayer.

Where family considerations have made burial unavoidable, you should avoid visiting the grave of your loved one. You know that he is not in the cemetery; so keep away from it. Pray for him in the sanctuary of your own home, for no other place is more sacred or appropriate. On his birthday, or any other significant anniversary, have a bunch of flowers, or a single rose or other flower that has special meaning for you, in remembrance of him—in front of his portrait if you have one. Let this be done at home and not in the graveyard, but only occasionally and not kept up as an everyday practice.

You should avoid wearing mourning or taking a mourning attitude which includes maintaining his room or his books, et cetera, "just as he left them," as some people do. There is no objection to keeping a few mementos if you are certain that you are not doing it in the spirit of mourning.

Now I reach the question of whether it is possible or not to communicate with those who have passed on into the next world. There are extremists on one side who say dogmatically that it is absolutely impossible to do so. Enthusiasts on the other side claim that they are in clear and intimate communication with their deceased friends frequently.

What is the truth? The truth is that communication does occasionally take place, but that it is far rarer than most believers in it suppose, and that it is always accomplished with considerable difficulty and uncertainty. The chief objection to the running after mediums that so many people practice is that it is really a running away from the responsibilities of this life. Professional mediums say that they seldom get a client who is happy, whose life is full of prosperity and self-expression. On the contrary, it is those whose lives here are frustrated and unhappy, irrespective of a particular bereavement, who are always trying to communicate with the next plane. Thus it becomes what is called in psychology an escape mechanism. Your business is to live here in this world while you are here; to face up to your problems here and to try to solve them; and to live in the next world when you get there.

There is a truly spiritual mode of communication from which nothing but good can come. It is this: Sit down quietly and remind yourself that the one God really is Omnipresent. Then reflect that your Real Self—the Divine Spark of you—is in the Presence of God now, and that the Real Self—the Divine Spark of your loved one—is also in the Presence of God. Do this for a few minutes every day, and sooner or later you will get a sense of communication. However, no detailed message will come, as a rule—only a definite and unmistakable sense that he knows you have thought of him and that he is thinking of you.

Now that you understand these things in some degree, it should be possible for you to go through life and to meet death with that "even mind" to which a modern seer referred. You should never be so completely wedded to any particular set of conditions—to a house, or a district, or a job, or a vocation, or to any earthly arrangement—that you cannot part from it without undue regret. You should not be dependent for your happiness or self-respect upon human praise or approval, though such things may be appreciated in their place. Your attitude should be:

I do my duty and enjoy myself where I am; I do my job and pass on—to another. I am going to live forever; in a thousand years from now I shall still be alive and active somewhere; in a hundred thousand years still alive and still active somewhere else; and so the events of today have only the importance that belongs to today. Always the best is yet to be. Always the future will be better than the present or the past because I am ever growing and progressing, and I am an immortal soul. I am the master of my fate. I greet the unknown with a cheer and press forward joyously, exulting in the Great Adventure.

Armed with this philosophy, and really understanding its power, you have nothing to fear in life or death—because God is all, and God is Good.

To all of what has gone before, Emmet Fox appends a note in which he says:

I would impress upon the reader that no written description can really do justice to the subject. It can but hint and suggest the truth.

However *correct* the itinerary of a journey may be, it is likely to seem somewhat dry and unattractive when read, since the beauty and joy of the new adventure must evade the written word.

The Stars

in

Their Courses ...*

There is another golden key to which Emmet Fox has called attention and which is a constant theme throughout the Bible although most Bible readers are rarely aware of it. The point is that people of ancient times were very astrological-minded. The Zodiac and its implications run all through the Bible; some in direct reference like the twelve tribes of Israel and their banners representing the twelve signs of the Zodiac, and others less direct, as, for instance, in the story of Creation in Genesis (1:14) where it says, "Let there be lights in the firmament of the heaven . . . and let them be for signs [zodiacal signs] and for seasons."

It is especially opportune that Emmet Fox discusses this at some length in his "Zodiac and the Bible— The End of the World"** with its predictions, some of which have already come true. I say it is especially relevant to the contemporary scene for we have

---

*Read Judg. 5, the story of a battle, and of deceit and treachery, and contemplate verse 20 in particular.
**See this chapter in the book *Alter Your Life.*

*entered a new era, the Aquarian Age. We find writers,
composers, and the general public keenly aware of
the New Age, although seldom do they realize that
Jesus himself alluded to it two thousand years ago.*

Emmet Fox points out:

The History of mankind proceeds in no haphazard or casual way, but through the unfoldment of a number of distinct periods or Ages. Each of these periods has its own characteristics, its own lessons to be learned, its own work to be done; and each one is quite fundamentally different in every respect from its predecessor and not a mere improvement or expansion of it. Each of these Ages is about two thousand one hundred and fifty years long; the passing from one such Age into another is always accompanied by both external and internal storm and stress such as the world has recently been going through. The last change took place a couple of thousand years ago, and the new world that formed itself from the melting pot was the Western Christian civilization that we know. This great enterprise, having worked itself out and fulfilled its mission, has now drawn to its close and the New Age is already upon us.

In connection with the coming and going of these different Ages it is necessary to be familiar with the natural phenomenon known as the Precession of the Equinoxes. It is not necessary that a student should possess any general knowledge of astronomy; it is sufficient to know that as we look out from our globe at the illimitable starry hosts that surround us, the axis of the earth seems to trace out a huge circle in the heavens every 26,000 years or thereabouts. This huge circle, which is known as the Zodiac, falls into twelve parts or sectors, and each part, or "Sign," as the Ancients called it, marks the passage of time that we occupy in working through one of our Ages.

This Zodiac is one of the most interesting of all the symbols that reveal the destiny of mankind. In fact, the Zodiac symbolizes the most fundamental thing in the nature of man. It is nothing less than the key to the history of the Human Race, of the psychology of the individual man, and of his regeneration or spiritual salvation. The Bible, which is of course the great fountain of Truth, has the Zodiac running through it from beginning to end. The twelve sons of Jacob who become the twelve tribes of the Old Testament, and the twelve Apostles of the New Testament, are, apart from their historical identity, special expressions of the twelve signs of the Zodiac. The marshaling of the Twelve Tribes of Israel in strict astronomical order in the great encampment in the wilderness is a leading example of this Zodiacal symbolism which the reader can check for himself.

We have now to ask ourselves the question, What is the real significance of the Zodiac? And in order to answer that question we must put others: What is the real reason of mankind being on the earth at all? What are we here for? What is it all about? Why are we born, and why do we die? Is there a reason or a pattern behind it all? And if so, what is it? And the answer to these questions, no doubt the most fundamental of all questions, is this: That we are here to learn the Truth of Being. That we are here to become self-conscious, self-governed entities, focal points of the Divine Mind, each expressing God in a new way. That is the object of our existence, and the only thing that we have to do to realize it is to get a better knowledge of God, because such knowledge is the answer to every problem.

In order to acquire that full understanding of all that God is, which will be man's complete salvation, man has to learn, piecemeal as it were, to know God in twelve different ways. It takes him two thousand years to learn each of these lessons. And so we can, if we like, think of our progress around the Zodiac as a series of twelve lessons which we have to learn about God.

Each of these lessons has a name which has been allotted to it for convenience. Everything must have a name, but as many of us know, names when rightly understood are often found to be symbolical of the things for which they stand, and the names of our lessons or "Signs" are no exception to the rule. The name of the last sign, the one which we have just left, was Pisces, or the Fishes. The one before that, which we left over two thousand years ago, was Aries, or the Ram. The one before that was Taurus, the Bull, and so forth. These names, be it noted, do not in the least refer to the physical shape of the constellations as seen in the sky. They refer to the innate character of the lesson that we have to learn at the particular time that is indicated by the Sign.

The New Age upon which we have now entered is called Aquarius—the Man with the Water Pot—and the Aquarian Age is going to be a completely new chapter in the history of mankind—not just a polishing up of the old Piscean ideas which most people make the mistake of regarding as the only possible ideas instead of being merely one of an infinite number of possible expressions.

Each of these Ages or ways of knowing God has a dominant quality or character of its own which distinguishes it from the other eleven. The quality which distinguishes the new Aquarian Age is called for convenience "Uranus," and in a general way all the activities and expressions of the Aquarian Age will be Uranian, and gives us a broad idea of the sort of thing that we may expect. Uranus is usually spoken of as a disrupter or smasher, but it must be remembered that this does not necessarily imply, as is too often assumed, real destruction. It is well that the less good should be destroyed if this means that the better is given an opportunity of taking its place.

Uranus is also spoken of as a symbol of democracy and freedom, and at other times it is referred to as standing for autocracy; but the actual truth is that Uranus stands neither for democracy nor autocracy as such, but for *individuality*. The free expression of individuality must mean true democracy in the sense that every human soul shall have an equal opportunity for self-expression as the thing that God intended it to be, and, on the other hand, as the master of its own fate and the captain of its own soul, it becomes the autocrat of its own life, answerable to God alone and unrestricted in its development by any tyrannical outside interference. That is Uranus.

As usual with Emmet Fox, what he says here is so true. As this chapter is being written on a terrace overlooking a beautiful beach along the Mediterranean, there are many young women who are sunbathing topless. The authorities have tried to discourage this trend, but without much success. The number increases rather than diminishes. Aside from the moral values involved, is this not an assertion of individual autocracy? As a matter of fact, this particular avenue of freedom of expression has been developing since the turn of the century. I am sure that most of us have seen photographs of male and female bathers of that period dressed from head to foot in bulky bathing suits that were more like anchors than swimsuits. But as we have gotten further into the Aquarian Age, individuals have rebelled against the outmoded ideas of the previous era. The present nudity is not merely a swing of the pendulum, but a continued emergence of the autocratic expression of the individual soul in this particular field.

As Emmet Fox points out:

What is happening and will continue to happen in the broad panorama of life is Uranian in nature. It means, for example, that in spite of temporary setbacks, dictatorships, collectivization, etc., the individual will at last emerge free. There are many factors under the Uranian influence that are helping this freeing of the individual. Electricity, which individualizes itself in many forms—light, radio, television, motors, refrigerators, heaters, and the whole galaxy of electronic marvels—has done more than any other material thing to liberate the human soul from the fetters of drudgery and physical limitations.

Radio is a particularly Uranian expression. It jumps barriers and boundaries and seeks out the individual. Internationally it laughs at frontiers, and thanks to its efforts, it will no longer be possible, however much reactionary authorities may desire it, to isolate any body of human beings from the common stock of human knowledge and human progress.

Television is another marvel of the Aquarian Age and seems to present entertainment and instruction to the masses, but being Uranian in nature, it is strictly an individual matter, and promoters and sponsors know it.

The Aquarian Age, in fact, is to be the age of personal freedom. It is no mere coincidence that its arrival marks the emancipation of women as a sex, and that in the present age the children too have at last been conceded rights as individuals, and are no longer regarded simply as the personal property of their parents.

Just as each Age is a special lesson that humanity has to learn about God, so in each Age there is a special outstanding teacher who teaches the lesson of that Age and demonstrates it in a complete and unmistakable manner. The great Race Teacher of the Age of Aries was Abraham. Abraham raised the standard of the One God, perfect, not made with hands, eternal in the heavens. Abraham when he received his enlightenment came straight out from idolatry and, forestalling Moses, said in effect: Know, O Israel, the Lord thy God is One God—Thou shalt have no other gods before Him—Thou shalt not make unto thyself graven images.

Abraham, having launched the new Age, that of Aries, or the Ram, passed into history, and his work went on with the usual ebb and flow characteristic of human activity. It should be noted that that Age is called symbolically the Age of the Ram, or Sheep, and that all through the Bible sheep are used to symbolize thoughts, and that the great outstanding lesson of the Bible is that we have to watch our thoughts, because whatever we think with conviction will come to us sooner or later. It is important to note in this connection how many of the great saints and heroes of the Bible were at one time shepherds. Jacob, Moses, David, Cyrus the Mede ("His Anointed"), and many of lesser importance all served an apprenticeship in the keeping of sheep—the right control of thought. And of the many titles that have been given to our Lord himself, he would prob-ably have preferred that of the Good Shepherd. Did he not say, "The Good Shepherd gives his life for his sheep?"

In all of this we see the influence of the Ariean lesson working itself out in the race thought. Egypt, in the Bible, stands for materialism, sin, sickness, and death ("Out of Egypt have I called my son"), and very significantly we are told that the Egyptians harbored an undying enmity and hatred for a shepherd. All this, of course, is not to be taken literally as a reflection upon the people who lived in the Nile Valley, and were no worse, if no better, than other men, but as a symbolical description of the working out of natural laws. It is an interesting fact that right down to the present day in the Jewish synagogues where the Ariean Age still lingers, the Ram's horn remains as a living symbol.

The Age which followed the Ariean Age, and from which we have recently emerged, and which might well be called the epoch of orthodox Christianity, is known as the Age of Pisces, or the Fishes. The great leader and prophet of that Age was, of course, Jesus Christ, and we know that in the early days of Christianity he was symbolized among his followers as a fish. The cross, the great emblem of Christianity in later times, was not used in the first days. People were then a little ashamed to think of the Master in connection with a Roman gibbet. In the catacombs of Rome and elsewhere we find inscriptions of the early Christians in which Jesus is referred to as the fish.

The Age of Pisces was constantly being announced in symbols by all sorts of people, many of whom realized not at all what it was that they were doing. The great medieval church, for instance, centered its authority, for practical purposes, in the bishop, and the distinguishing symbol of a bishop is, of course, the mitre. And what is the mitre but a fish's head worn as a headdress. Jesus said, "I will make you fishers of men," and actually his first disciples were fishermen, just as the Old Testament leaders were shepherds.

All through the Bible, and throughout the old occult tradition in general, the fish stands as a symbol of wisdom, and wisdom is then understood as the technical term for the knowledge of the Allness of God and of the power of prayer.

As Emmet Fox has already pointed out, people often use symbols without really knowing what they signify. In the present instance, there are many people who say "fish is brain food" in perhaps happy ignor-

ance that fish symbolize wisdom and have nothing to do with food or other materiality.

As previously mentioned, the present era, the Aquarian Age, is the Age of the Man with the Water Pot ("Seek ye a man bearing a pot of water"—Luke 22:10), and who is the man with the water pot? The gardener, of course, and so the interpretative symbol of the New Age is to be the Gardener. Man having graduated as a Shepherd, and as a Fisherman, now becomes a Gardener, and this title nicely expresses the kind of work that he has to do in his new role. We have reached the stage when the lesson of the need for thought control having been learned, and the *Santa Sophia*, or Holy Wisdom, having been contacted and appreciated, the two things must be united mentally in our everyday practice.

Modern science is making some of its greatest strides in the realm of psychology, so that indeed psychology may today be called the handmaid of metaphysics, and psychology is insisting more and more that the conscious and the subconscious minds stand almost exactly in the relationship of gardener and garden. The gardener sows his seed in the soil that he has prepared; he waters the ground and, as far as possible, he selects a site upon which the sun will shine; he does not, however, try to make the seed grow. He leaves that to Nature. So, in spiritual treatment or Scientific Prayer, we speak the Word, but we leave it to the Divine Power to make the demonstration. "I have planted; Apollos watered; but God gave the increase" (Paul).

At this stage the question naturally presents itself, Who is, or who is to be, the great teacher and prophet of our new Aquarian Age? It seems that there is no lack of candidates for the position. All over the world sundry people are laying claim to this high office, or their followers are claiming it for them. No time need be wasted over this sort of thing. Did not the Master warn us that false Christs would arise who would deceive, if it were possible, the very elect.

The wonderful fact is that now, after all these thousands and thousands of years of upward striving, we have at last reached the stage where humanity is ready to do without personal prophets of any kind, and to contact the Living God at first hand for itself.

And so the Great World Teacher of the New Age is not to be any man or woman, or any textbook, or any organization, but the Indwelling Christ that each individual is to find and contact for himself—again the Uranian autocracy of the individual.

It takes humanity about 26,000 years to go through this class of twelve lessons about God, which we call the Zodiac. But we have been through that class many times already— remember that the race is far older than most people think —and we shall have to go through it many times more, but each time we go through the same lessons at a much higher level, garnering a different *quality* of knowledge, for it is not an endless circle, but an upward reaching spiral.

So now we see that the Zodiac is really one of the great cosmic symbols, perhaps the greatest of them all, a diagram of the unfoldment of the human soul, and not the mere physical fact of the Precession of the Equinoxes. It is not just a kind of circular railroad track for fortune telling, but one of the deepest mysteries of the soul—and that is why it runs through the Bible from Genesis to Revelation.

As has been quoted so often, Jesus says, "Know the Truth, and the Truth shall make you free." If we know the Truth in this new Aquarian Age—and practice it—we shall sweep forward in the grand march of humanity, learning the new lessons, rejoicing in the new work, and triumphing in its triumphs. As the old landmarks disappear one by one beneath the rising tide of the new life, we shall go boldly on, knowing that the best is yet to be, and as the Bible says, "Eye hath not seen, nor ear heard, neither have entered into the heart of man the things which God hath prepared for them that love Him" (1 Cor. 2:9).

Part Two

Reminiscences

Arrival

Of all the golden keys which Emmet Fox gave to the world, the greatest one was Emmet Fox himself. He opened a new way of life for millions of people and was the means of channeling healing to thousands of others. His faith in the power of constructive thinking and its ability to change lives continues to affect millions through his published writings.

The time was early in 1931, and the place London. Emmet Fox knew a change was coming in his life and he decided then that it was time to take an extended vacation. He had been toying with the idea of going to Russia as he thought that country was in the throes of an interesting political experiment, and Russia itself was beginning to open its doors to the outside world. As was his way whenever any important decision had to be made, he prayed at length for guidance. His answer, he recalled, was a voice saying to him, "Go West; see America first." He never did get to Russia but years later, "Reincarnation," one of his most popular booklets, was printed in the Russian language in the United States by the Unity School of Christianity, and it eventually found its way into Russia where it was reprinted in magazines.

In making his decision to come to the United States, Emmet Fox brought to America an enrichment it had not known before, and which in time spread to the rest of the world as well. Little did anyone realize in the summer of 1931 when Emmet Fox stepped off the ship in New York that one of the greatest mystics and religious teachers of this century had arrived. As a matter of fact, probably not more than a dozen people in America had ever heard of him at that time.

He came to the United States on a six-month visa and like "the man who came to dinner," stayed for twenty years. Shortly after his arrival Florence Scovel Shinn, who had met him in London, invited him to take her meetings at the Unity Center in New York while she went on vacation. Emmet Fox appeared on the platform without any previous announcement. It was obvious some people in the audience were disappointed and several walked out—undoubtedly to their own loss. However, the same process happened in reverse several years later when other commitments took him out of town and he asked another speaker to substitute for him. By that time huge crowds were attending. Seven hundred persons walked out when the other speaker appeared!

But at this first meeting those who stayed had a rare treat. As one woman wrote, "He was so marvelous that the next week we went to the meeting very early, for we felt there would be a crowd. There was! Unity opened every room in their suite and even put chairs in the halls to accommodate as many as possible."

At this particular time the Church of the Healing Christ in New York needed a new minister. Emmet Fox was invited to undertake the pastorate of this well-established Church, and from the very first Sunday he was a great success. The Church was then holding services in the Biltmore Hotel and under his leadership it had to move constantly to larger quarters within the hotel.

At this point his visa expired and he obtained another six-month renewal, and kept this renewal process going for two years. At the end of that time the numbers attending the Sunday services had climbed to a couple of thousand, but because of legal restrictions no further extensions could be had on his passport. He was already recognized as an outstanding religious leader in America, and through the helpful intervention of the then two U.S. senators from New York, Robert W. Wagner and Dr. Royal S. Copeland, Emmet Fox was able to reenter the country after the summer vacation in 1933 as a permanent resident of the United States.

The work continued to grow by leaps and bounds; the large ballroom at the Hotel Biltmore became too small. In passing, it is interesting to note how the Church happened to hold its services at the Biltmore in the first place, as it demonstrates that crass commercialism does not always win out. When the board of trustees of the Church were looking for new quarters because its old meeting place, the original Waldorf Astoria Hotel, was being demolished to make room for the towering Empire State Building, they approached the management of the Biltmore. Several meetings with the top executives took place, and some were against housing the Church, arguing that it would be an unprofitable commercial venture. At the final meeting the famous John M. Bowman, president of the Bowman Biltmore hotels, was present. He listened to the arguments and then said to his staff, "Gentlemen, it seems to me that we have everything in this hotel but God." The Church was in.

The
Work

From the beginning the Church experienced growing pains. In June 1933 Emmet Fox sent this greeting to the members and friends of the Church:

"This service completes our activities for the season 1932–33. It has been a year of vigorous growth and progress. The Church membership has largely increased and the general attendance has grown steadily from week to week. It will be noted that more than once we have had to move our quarters from one part of the hotel to another, but this has been caused by the need for more room and is a tribute to the success of the work.

"Many striking demonstrations have been reported to me, and most of us feel that we have made a very definite advance upon our former selves of June 1932. A number of remarkable healings have occurred during our meetings but what I consider to be still more important is that many people have demonstrated both in bodily health and in affairs by their own *personal* work. The power of self-healing is the only guarantee that one really understands the teaching. The circulation of our various booklets and publications has greatly increased and this is a matter of

congratulation because the written word is almost the best
way of spreading the message at the present time.

"May the summer intermission be an opportunity for
mental stock-taking and a general reorganization of your
spiritual life. It is well that there should be such periods
when the mind can digest and assimilate the food which it
has been receiving."

Recessing for the three months of summer was an established annual procedure. E.F. often said, "You need a rest;
and so do I." But he never did really rest. The hiatus
simply meant that he took his activities elsewhere, to un-
earth new facets of Truth where he could find them, and
to give life-sustaining instruction to people across the
country and around the world. Yet he always returned re-
freshed and renewed in the fall.

E.F. was a tireless worker. "Do not waste time," he said.
"What we call 'time' represents the very substance of your
existence. The hours and the days, the months and the
years, are soul substance, either efficiently employed in
building up a successful and glorious life for you, or
wasted and lost."

At one of the International New Thought Alliance
conventions Dr. Ernest Holmes* asked, "Dr. Fox, how is it
that at the end of every June you can close up the Church,
go away for three months, come back in October, and you
have the crowd right back with you?"

E.F. replied with a chuckle, "I carry them in my pocket."

To which Dr. Joseph Murphy,** who was also present,
added, "He keeps them in the pocket of his mind."

Emmet Fox was always crowd conscious. Yet he never
tried to hold on to people. He would say to the congrega-

*Founder of the Church of Religious Science, Los Angeles.
** Minister of the Church of Divine Science, Los Angeles.

tion, "There are a number of good centers and churches in the city. While I am gone, if you find someone else where you can get more help, you must stay there." Perhaps a few did, but there always seemed to be more people at the meetings when he returned after the summer recess.

Location made no difference, for no matter where he spoke, a crowd gathered. In 1940, at the I.N.T.A. convention in San Francisco, the large ballroom at the Palace Hotel was packed beyond its capacity. At our own meetings in New York, the crowds were often so large that people who arrived late had to sit on the platform or on the floor. Ladies in expensive mink coats would roll them into a ball and sit on them wherever they could find space.

In London politics years before, E.F. was crowd conscious. His father was an M.D. and a Member of Parliament. When the Liberal Party's regular speakers could not rally a crowd, E.F. would be sent for because even then he had a charisma that attracted people.

Blanche and I had a chance to see this phenomenon at work during one of the trips the three of us made to Yosemite National Park in California. We were having breakfast in the large dining room of the lodge at Glacier Point which overlooks the majestic El Capitan. That year the play *Green Pastures*—a show well ahead of its time— was the rave of Broadway. Blanche and I had not seen it, and in this exquisite setting high up in the Sierras, E.F. was telling us about it enthusiastically, describing "de Lawd with his big fat cigar smoking away as he played God." As the story unfolded we noticed that people from other tables were discretely gathering around us. Waitresses stopped serving and listened. I pointed out to E.F. that there was a large audience behind him—enough to start a metaphysical meeting—and as he turned around they burst into applause.

In New York, as the attendance at meetings grew and grew, we continually had to change locations to accommodate the numbers. From the Biltmore we moved to the Hotel Astor with its larger ballroom; then finally to the Hippodrome which was the largest auditorium in New York City with the exception of Madison Square Garden. It was not unusual to have five to six thousand people at services on Wednesday evenings and Sunday mornings. On special occasions such as Easter the figure reached eight thousand, and police were needed to direct the flow of traffic.

The meetings soon attracted notice from the press. No public relations staff was necessary as word of mouth and faithful attendance were eloquent enough. *Newsweek* featured an article with the headline, "Preacher Uses Hotel Ballroom to Popularize Prayer," and commented, "Every Sunday the preacher, Emmet Fox, pounds home the same vital message: 'Prayer does change things!' " When reporters asked E.F. why he held his meetings in ballrooms and theaters, he replied, "I couldn't get some men into church with a shotgun, but they'll come to a hotel."

Walter Winchell, the well-known New York columnist, wrote in his inimitable fashion, "Two new religious movements are attracting plenty. Emmet Fox, who a year ago held his meets in a hotel, now turns them away from the Hippodrome and the Manhattan Opera House!"

The unique quality about the Hippodrome was that because of its vast size it could house the Ringling Brothers Circus which appeared there every spring. The smell of the circus never left the building from one visit to the next. However, that turned out to be in our favor, for it served to remind people that what Emmet Fox was giving was not some offbeat teaching but, like circuses ancient or modern, a part of the fabric of life.

We had as a member of the board of trustees Earl Chapin May, author of the best-selling *From Rome to Ringling*. May and E.F. became good friends, for they both valued what the circus had to offer. When it came to town, E.F. urged people to go to the circus, emphasizing its youthifying effects, and said that the best way to enjoy it was to see it through the eyes of a child: "If you don't have a child of your own, beg, borrow or steal one and go to the circus."

Emmet Fox got to know the performers and the backstage side of circus life. He often used stories about what he saw there in his sermons. One had a striking effect: A woman who in her dressing room seemed plain and old, became a glamorous young performer when she rode into the arena on her horse like a queen! As the band played a stirring theme and the audience burst into applause, all the years fell away. A dramatic example of the power of mind.

At least once during the season E.F. gave a cocktail-dinner party for the circus performers. It was delightful for us to sit next to people who only an hour before were "flying through the air with the greatest of ease." Yet they also had problems like everyone else once they left fantasy and returned to reality, and it was the help E.F. could give them that interested him most.

People came to the meetings to have their spiritual batteries recharged. Dorothy Giles, writing in *Cosmopolitan*, said, "America's soul clinics had taken me to one of Emmet Fox's Sunday meetings. There I had seen some four thousand New Yorkers of every walk in life—lawyers, teachers, bank clerks and bank presidents, stenographers, debutantes and Park Avenue dowagers."

The names of the people who attended read like a Who's Who listing. The famous restaurateur, Patricia

Murphy, came with her assistant and decorated the platform at the Hippodrome with flowers many Sunday mornings. Charles Schwab, the steel industry executive, often attended on Wednesday evenings. On one occasion he remarked, "What a wonderful thing it would be for the country and for industry if we could get a man like this in the steel business!" Later, when we moved to Carnegie Hall, the musical conductor, Mitropoulos, sometimes attended the Wednesday or Friday noon meetings, after which he would go into rehearsal with his orchestra. When time permitted, E.F. and I would stay to listen to the performance.

After awhile we discovered that in addition to people from the theater, business, professional, and political worlds, a number of divines from other faiths were also attending meetings. Then we noticed that the announcements of their Sunday sermon topics in the religious advertising columns of the newspapers took on a more constructive and metaphysical aspect.

Through the active interest of the well-known actress Paula Stone, Emmet Fox was heard on radio for a time, and a special edition of his booklet, "Alter Your Life," was published for the thousands of listeners who requested it. The program was moderately successful because of the rigid censorship regulations in effect in those days. It was necessary to submit a copy of the completed lecture before air time for approval by the radio station. This form of presentation was not E.F.'s style and it erased some of the natural sparkle and delicious humor that he had on a public platform where his entire notes (if any) consisted of four or five words on an index card. He was at his inspirational best as an extemporaneous speaker.

Nevertheless E.F. realized the tremendous power of radio and said to me, "I look forward to the day when the strict rules of censorship will be lifted and we, as well as others, will carry on the work almost entirely by radio. That will be the best way to get the message to the largest number of people." Another prediction of his was that the metaphysical approach toward teaching religion would be integrated more and more into the orthodox churches as the new generation of religious leaders became aware of the great potential in scientific—affirmative—prayer, and the need for healing as Jesus demonstrated it.

Both of these predictions have come true. We see religious programs proliferating at a great rate on both radio and television. Many orthodox churches include healing work as an integral part of their services. Some have established spiritual healing clinics. Ministers integrate as much metaphysical teaching as possible within the tenets of the religion they espouse. They are returning to what E.F. called "the practical Christianity of Jesus Christ without dogma or creed."

HEALING

His work was divided broadly into four parts: lectures, classes, consultation, and healing. E.F. considered healing the most important: "Healing is an essential part of the Jesus Christ teaching. If you are coming to the meetings and reading the books, and you are not getting healings, at least in some departments of your life, then you definitely have not made your contact with God."

Emmet Fox, who was the channel for healing so many people all over the world, said that he did some of his best praying on the busy streets of New York, London, or Paris, and while riding in taxicabs and subway trains. However, he added that setting aside a quiet time each day is the better plan for most people, who then can, in such a relaxed atmosphere, turn to God in thought. He believed that some people were born with a natural gift of healing and that others cultivated the power of healing in themselves through long hours of prayer, meditation, and practice.

There were occasions when those who came to him for the healing of their own problems, he worked with and developed into healers of others. These he selected intuitively. His gifts gave him the ability to read the hearts of other people, and to perceive in some a healing power of which they themselves were not aware. All they needed to realize this was the confidence in themselves that he was able to ignite. Sometimes he would have such a person take on a case that he was working with. In this way it not only allowed for practice in healing but served as a testing ground for ability. One requirement that he was firm about was that when treating, the healer always mention the patient's first name. He considered this a person's dominant tone or note, and that it was their "I Am" in this incarnation.

He also believed that people who felt deeply troubled or worried should call on those who had been close to them in this life and who had since passed on. He referred to this as the real "communion of saints"—people on the same spiritual level working together from both sides of the "silken" curtain.

He believed in the bodily healing value of the laying on of hands, especially when placed at the nape of the neck. But he cautioned that the act should be done with an acknowledgment that the divine Healing Presence was going forth through one's hands. In his own practice of this technique he sometimes touched people to gain a sense of their spiritual response—as if he might physically touch their aura which he considered a spiritual color program of health or disease, harmony or anxiety.

He believed that all healing came from God and that

the highest form of it was through affirmative prayer and contemplation, i.e., just *thinking* about God. Yet he also respected the medical profession. At times he would not undertake a physical healing until a patient first consulted a doctor. In these cases he felt the patient would be relieved of much anxiety by learning from the doctor that the ailment was not nearly so serious as anticipated. He would counsel the patient to pray for the doctor as well as for himself, and to bless all who were connected with the case.

E.F.'s ability to heal people and to better their physical condition became well known to many doctors, and there were a number of instances where physicians advised patients to go to Emmet Fox. Of those who came from all walks of life, some were healed in one or two visits; others came nine or ten times. It all depended on how tenaciously a person held on to the problem.

In his healing work he followed no particular technique and his methods varied with the problem at hand. Sometimes he would slowly pace up and down in a room while the patient was talking, treating as he walked. Other times he let the whole story be told before doing any treating at all. On occasion he had to root out the real difficulty, especially in situations where inharmonious family and marital relationships prevailed. In some instances two or three members of the same family were coming to him for treatment simultaneously without one knowing about the other. He would say to me, "We have to keep these in airtight compartments." When the healing was accomplished he cautioned the patient, "Tell no one for a while until the healing has had time to 'jell.' "

In his healing gift E.F. had a special and outstanding quality. He had an uncanny way of isolating the essentials and seeing the difficulty in its true light and proportions.

This permitted a great sense of peace and calm to come into the patient. I do not mean to imply that the difficulty was always cleared up immediately but that it no longer seemed to be out of proportion. His advice was often unorthodox, as in the case of a woman with whom he was working for some time. She called him one evening for urgent help. His advice was, "Leave that man tonight. Take your children and go to a hotel." This counsel was given in spite of the fact that he believed separation and divorce was the last solution to marital difficulties. Indeed, he felt that divorce solved no problems unless one changed the mental attitude that had resulted in such a drastic resolution. Otherwise, the next marriage could easily fall into the same pattern. He trusted his intuition, and his advice and guidance flowed from it. This approach did not always coincide with a rational point of view. Yet his advice turned out to be sound and brought happiness and release to many whom he advised, as it did to this woman and her children.

Another unique case of healing was that of a well-known singer who was selected to sing at the inauguration of Franklin D. Roosevelt. She delighted in the honor until the day drew near for the trip to Washington, when she suddenly developed a sore throat. She came to the Friday noon meeting and made an appointment to see E.F. There was such a long list that she did not get in to see him until 5:30 P.M. She asked E.F. to treat for her throat.

But he said instead, "Why don't you forgive your parents?"

Astonished, she did admit that she felt an animosity toward them for what she thought was good reason. But she replied, "Yes I can and I do."

He answered, "Your voice is going to be fine. When you sing, believe that healing goes out through your voice."

Everything went beautifully at the inauguration and she still has an autographed picture of the President and Mrs. Roosevelt on her piano in her villa in Key West as a happy reminder of the occasion.

Of course, these are only two examples of the hundreds, yes thousands, of people who came to E.F. for treatment and consultation over the years, but at least they can give some indication of the way he handled people.

His healing power was also at work during lectures and sermons. He advised all persons in the creative arts to realize that healing went out through their work in the same way he had explained it to the singer. He so thoroughly believed this himself that there was hardly a time when at least two or three people left a meeting feeling that their problems had been solved. He often remarked that one effective healing would demonstrate more to an individual than reading a dozen books or attending twenty lectures. People took him at his word, and so after every meeting (except Sundays) dozens of people would line up to see him for spiritual advice. Very often after a Wednesday evening meeting, there were so many people waiting that we would not get home until three or four o'clock in the morning, and on one snowy night in the middle of winter it was 8 A.M.

E.F. was not influenced by status. He mentioned a number of times how amused he was with people who bragged about their ancestry, and observed how "seldom anyone was related to the hangman." He said that such people were like a potato—the best part of them was underground. After one noonday meeting a socialite expressed a desire to see him, and I told her there would be quite a wait. She gave me her card—her name was vaguely familiar—and said she was sure Dr. Fox would see her right away if I took the card in. I did so and E.F. came out and said to her, "I recognize your need and will be glad to see you if you can wait until I see the others who already have their names on the list and have their needs too." She immediately calmed down and waited. After a couple of hours passed during which she got a little fidgety, she finally got in to see him. When she came out she was a changed woman. All the tension and belligerency had vanished, and she thanked me profusely for having arranged the appointment— although I had done very little.

While he was instrumental in bringing healings to others, he always found himself the most difficult person to treat for. In fact, he said he had more difficulty with E.F. than with any other person he knew. He arrived one day at the Manhattan Opera House with no voice. He said in a hoarse whisper over the microphone to a crowd of more than five thousand people, "If you want to hear a lecture tonight you will have to practice what you've learned. Treat for me right now." He sat down and in complete silence prayed with them. A few minutes later he returned to the microphone with his voice completely healed, and delivered one of his best lectures.

After the Wednesday and Friday noon lectures he usually answered written questions that were handed in. These were always worthwhile because they reached the core of people's problems and aspirations. During World War II there were many questions about men in the service, such as, "How can I help a man who is in the war." His answer: "Get fear out of your own heart. Treat yourself. Get that fear out of *your* heart and he will be safe. Don't ask me how; that is too complicated; but he will. Pray until you feel satisfied that God is with you. That is the very best treatment of all."

Another typical example: "Can another person's thoughts affect me? His answer: "Only your own thoughts can affect you. Of course, if you dislike the other person and think he wants to hurt you, that will hurt you, but it is your own belief. See the Christ in him and that will free both him and yourself."

Still another example: "What can I do to help my husband who is very nervous about an upcoming examination?" His answer: "You can help your husband by getting out of your own thought the idea that he is nervous and evidently highly strung. Realize peace and harmony, and then claim it for him. And when he has to sit for the examination, claim that Divine Intelligence works through him—and believe it!"

PERSONAL

On May 21, 1941, Blanche and I witnessed the ceremony during which Emmet Fox became an American citizen. It was a complete surprise to us. We knew he loved America and its people but we had no idea he had undertaken the steps required for citizenship. As he was handed his papers, he took a small American flag from his pocket and waved it with joy. He told us then that he wanted for some years to make the United States his home, that "it was only natural" he should become part of this great nation. He said he always knew he had an American soul and that one day he would explain to us what that meant. But for the moment the three of us went out and celebrated.

Some weeks later we went on a "mysterious" journey with him along the Hudson River. We soon found ourselves standing before a house in Cohoes, New York. E.F. revealed that this was where his mother and father originally settled when they came to the New World. It was where his sister Nora was born, and where, as he put it, he was conceived, and why he claimed he had an American soul. But before his birth occurred his mother became intensely homesick for her native Ireland, and his father decided to return there. As a result Emmet was born in Cork, Ireland, on July 30, 1886. Later the family moved to London, where his father reestablished his medical practice and eventually became a Member of Parliament under the Liberal Party banner.

In one of our conversations the question of marriage surfaced. He said thoughtfully, "I have thought about it more than once, and I realize that I could have lived a more normal and perhaps a happier life, but I have always felt that the work was so important that I had to forego these things and devote all my energies and time to getting out the message." Yet he always enjoyed female company, had many women friends, and lots of lady admirers.

One of the duties of the trustees of the Church was to escort him home after the lectures, as there were always women waiting for him when he left the auditorium. At first he was quite open about his address and travel plans but this openness turned into an embarrassment. To find two or three women waiting for him in the lobby of his hotel when he returned in the evening became a common occurrence. Once, when he mentioned he was sailing on a certain ship for Europe, he found his cabin lavishly decorated with flowers. He had the steward remove them, saying that it looked more like a funeral parlor than a stateroom. Having learned his lesson the hard way, E.F. became more secretive about his whereabouts.

Yet he always put women on a pedestal, saying that the more women were emancipated the more civilization and democracy advanced. He cited examples of how Jesus and his apostles put women on an equal basis with men: Jesus' friendship with Martha and Mary; his forgiving Mary Magdalene in her battle for survival with the rabble of the town after being caught in adultery; and his sermon to the woman at the well in Samaria in which he laid down the basic principle of man's relationship to God: "God is a Spirit: and they that worship Him must worship Him in Spirit and in Truth" (John 4:24).

At one of the meetings a young woman said to Blanche, "How I envy your sitting next to Dr. Fox on those long journeys across country." We did not disillusion her by explaining that E.F. always sat next to me in the front seat.

Like W. John Murray* before him, Emmet Fox took a very practical approach to life. When someone came to him seeking spiritual aid, and he sensed an acute financial need present as well, he gave assistance. And since he was devoted to the expansion of the metaphysical teaching, he also helped a number of the teachers and leaders in that field anywhere he found them, as he did with Georgiana Tree West. She was the leader of the Unity Center in New York, and at the time was in the hospital. It was June and we were leaving for Europe in a few days. We visited Mrs. West, and E.F. assured her of his prayers and that these would continue until he felt certain that she was completely recovered (which she did). Then he added, "At times like this I realize that anxiety as to how the bills can be met retards the demonstration. I want to leave this with you." He placed an envelope on the table next to her bed, and we left. Mrs. West told me months later how amazed and grateful she was at his generosity. Inside the envelope were ten one hundred dollar bills.

Mailing a hundred dollar bill to someone in need was his favorite way of sending gifts, and included in the envelope was his blessing that the bill would increase and

* Founder of the Church of the Healing Christ in 1906.

multiply. He never tried to accumulate money or possessions. He said, "I need only one apartment; I can eat only one meal at a time." He once refused an increase in salary, and never asked for money for himself or the Church. Both needs were met by a consciousness of prosperity on his part and that of the congregation. Indeed, a consciousness of prosperity was a keynote in the teaching, for the meetings were built up through the depression years.

THEORIES AND IDEAS

E.F. and I often talked about abstract theories. One time, as we drove across the prairies at sixty miles an hour, I said to him that it seemed strange to experience the bushes at the side of the road as rushing past us—or we them—at great speed, and yet the houses and trees in the distance seemed to be moving the same way we were.

He replied, "Nothing moves and nothing stands still." I waited for an explanation of this seeming paradox. He continued, "Einstein and the mathematicians might be able to explain it better, mathematically.* We are heading for Nebraska. It will take us so many hours and minutes and seconds to get there. If we could say that the car was at any particular point in this journey, then the car would not be moving, it would be standing still, yet we know it isn't. No matter how small an interval of time we use, the same thing would be true.

"I believe the whole of existence is a state of consciousness in the Mind of God, being re-created perhaps a billion times a second. We might compare it to the electric sign with moving lights. It seems as if the light were traveling

---

*Later when we had an appointment with Einstein in Princeton, this seemed to be confirmed.

around the sign but we know that is an illusion caused by each bulb lighting up in turn for a fraction of a second—what we might call metaphysically 'flashes of consciousness.' The same thing is true with motion pictures. The actors seem to move, but actually the movies are a series of still pictures.

"It is because life is a state of consciousness that spiritual healing is possible. The difference between Jesus with his instantaneous demonstrations and others who may have to spend some time in prayer before the healing takes place, is that Jesus had a complete awareness of perfection. When he could motivate that belief in others, the healing followed. The person was 're-created in wholeness.' "

E.F. had a theory too about those who have recently passed on. He felt that they sometimes made their presence known to a friend or relative by producing an odor of roses in a room. He explained that this mode of communication was easier for the departed one to use than some other means which might be more effective later on. Such communication had happened to him several times in his life and he was able usually to get a sense of who the person was. He shared this knowledge with his private classes but always cautioned the students not to make a fetish of it: "Develop spiritually and all these things will come to you."

Another theory he held and discussed during his lectures was that in the future it would be possible to think oneself to a desired place and then be able to find oneself there. However, he would add in his inimitable humor, "In the meantime, until we attain that state of awareness, it is easier to hop into a taxi or train and pay the fare."

He felt that humankind had only begun to sense the true powers resident in the Mind of God and therefore in the mind of the individual: "There is only one Mind in the universe, Divine Mind, and we are all individualizations of that—undivided parts. This is the true 'image and likeness.' "

He felt too that experiments in ESP, psychokinetics, cybernetics, etc. were footprints on the sands of time, leading man to new mental and spiritual discoveries. He said of the fourth dimension that it could be apprehended mathematically and that in it time and space become inextricably bound together: "That is only the first step in the expanded consciousness, for in Truth the universe, both physical and mental, is multidimensional."

He believed: "There are many other races of beings besides the human race. We know only a tiny corner of the universe. There are beings who were once human and who have now advanced far beyond our comprehension. There are entities called angels who can be sent by God at certain times but their appearances in this world are very, very rare, and they do not come unless sent. However, angels never were human."

His
Publishers

Although Emmet Fox lectured to audiences of five to six thousand people twice a week—on Wednesday evenings at the Manhattan Opera House and Sunday mornings at the Hippodrome—which was thought to be at that time the largest continuous congregation in the United States, it is a fact now that his biggest audience is the readers of his books. To this end his publishers have performed a valuable service. Harper & Row estimate that over the years there have been twelve million readers of their editions. His writings have been the major method of helping people throughout the world.

When Emmet Fox first came to America, his writings, such as "The Golden Key," "Alter Your Life," and others, were privately published as booklets and distributed. His famous interpretation of the Sermon on the Mount was originally done this way. However, publication work grew in such proportions after a few years that it became evident an established publishing house would have to take over. And so it was that Harper & Brothers (now Harper & Row) came into the picture. Under their expert handling a new edition of *The Sermon on the Mount* reached bestseller rating on nonfiction lists, and it has remained a best seller on religious lists ever since. By 1940, just a few years after the book appeared, Harper had published nineteen editions.

Edward Larocque Tinker, distinguished historian and book critic, wrote in the *New York Times Book Review* of March 31, 1940: "This book is a condensed, distilled essence of years of Bible and metaphysical study—a practical hand-book of spiritual development. . . . In explaining the manifold benefits of perfect understanding of Jesus' teachings, Dr. Fox concisely and without a trace of sensationalism gives his readers a profound outlook upon life, and an absolutely fresh scale of values which the Sermon on the Mount presents to mankind.

"In these days of rampant prejudices and frantic apprehensions we need to be reminded, in Dr. Fox's calm, well-chosen words, of the Forgotten Secret of Personal Power; this Power which is at once the source of all things—transforming itself into prosperity, inspiration and health. Any one of us can call it into use.

"In the light of scientific Christianity, thoughts are the weapons with which to combat poverty, unhappiness or lack of any kind. . . . Since we are molding our own destinies day by day, our right reactions to experiences are the secret of success; for we attract to ourselves sickness or health, riches or poverty, friends or enemies, entirely in accordance with our own thoughts.

"This is in essence what Jesus taught and it reverses all conventional or orthodox religion, for it turns our gaze from the outside to the inside for help—from man and his works to God.

"The substance of Dr. Fox's purpose is to show that everyone has troubles, ill health and all the rest of it, but that down the ages certain people have attained mastery over these misfortunes and through their own efforts have been able to lead lives of unbroken happiness."

To quote from another source, Albert Linn Lawson reported in the *Christian Herald*: "Not in a long time have I come across anything that surprised and delighted me so much as *The Sermon on the Mount* by Emmet Fox. . . . It would seem that the many, many volumes written about the Sermon on the Mount would well-nigh have said all that human tongue could say about it. Far from so! Dr. Fox has opened my eyes, and will, I feel sure, likewise open the eyes of everyone who reads his book.

"His inescapable conclusion is stated with overwhelming effect . . . that now, if we are to 'come of age,' spiritually, we have not merely to conform outwardly to outer rules, but that change in the inner man, too, is indispensable—a lesson the world seems in danger of forgetting."

Harper wrote to the book trade: "The extraordinary sales record of *The Sermon on the Mount* has been achieved with very little effort on the part of either publisher or book trade." The book spoke for itself. In other words, *readers* of the book promoted its phenomenal success because they found that it really was a key to successful living.

Articles by Emmet Fox began to appear in publications such as *Cosmopolitan, Harper's Bazaar, Divine Science Monthly* (now *Aspire*), and Unity magazines.

With the United States entering World War II in December 1941, serious paper shortages developed as time went on, and publishers were forced to distribute what paper supply they had on an allotment basis among all their titles. However, the increasing demand for the *Sermon* was so steady that this ration plan would not work, and an interesting solution was evolved. Another publishing firm, Grosset & Dunlap, had more paper on hand than was needed and that firm agreed to undertake the publication of *The Sermon on the Mount* for the duration of the paper shortage. Fred Becker, sales director at Harper for many years, wrote me: "Three years later when we exercised our right to take the book back, they were quite unhappy [to give it up] after selling a half million copies during the war book boom."

As the book became more and more popular, Harper suggested that Emmet Fox appear at autographing parties in department stores around the country. At first E.F. was reluctant to commercialize his work in this way, but when Fred Becker and Eugene Exman, editor-manager of Harper's Religious Books Department, convinced him that it would spread the teaching and help even greater numbers of people, he relented.

At one of the sales conferences where promotion for the book was being planned with the executive and sales personnel, each was stating what he would contribute to the book, one this, another that, and so on. E.F. listened with amusement, and then remarked, "I can't help but feel that the author makes a contribution too!"

He did appear at a number of autographing parties in major cities around the country. Fred Becker, who accompanied him, said, "One of the exciting things for me was to be with Emmet Fox and see the love and devotion of his followers; and some of the most important buyers in the country were really amazed."

At one autographing party E.F. appeared with Margaret Mitchell, author of *Gone with the Wind*. Although their books were poles apart, they really had a good time together. With his never-failing sense of humor, he commented to the audience that it was only fitting and proper to have a minister on the program to balance the proceedings!

When autographing books Emmet Fox often prefaced his signature with the quotation, " 'There is nothing good or bad but thinking makes it so.'—Shakespeare." He felt this statement by the great Initiate summed up the essence of his own teaching that thought is the key to destiny.

Emmet Fox had a deep feeling about spreading the metaphysical teaching to other countries and underwrote the translation and publication of a French and a Spanish edition of the *Sermon*. After the war Unity sought to lift the spirit of the German people through publishing and distributing in that language an edition of the *Sermon*. At present there are editions of his writings in France, Mexico, Brazil, and Greece.

Unity also published two booklets, "The Mental Equivalent" and "Life Is Consciousness," which are the substance of several lectures Emmet Fox delivered at Unity in Kansas City. These, too, have reached vast numbers and have also been the means for healing and changing lives. Dr. Jack Holland, the well-known professor at San Jose State College in California, has publicly testified on several occasions that he received a healing of a serious illness by reading and concentrating on "The Mental Equivalent" even though he never personally met Emmet Fox.

In the early years many out-of-town readers came to Harper's office in New York expecting, naïvely perhaps, to find Emmet Fox there and "to ask him a question." It was Eleanor Jordan, one of the staff at Harper's who was thoroughly familiar with the books, who acted as surrogate for E.F. and directed the visitor to E.F.'s office. And I am sure Miss Jordan helped many of them along the spiritual path.

Other works appeared in time and these, too, became best sellers in their turn: *Find and Use Your Inner Power, Power Through Constructive Thinking, Make Your Life Worth While,* and so on.

Since E.F.'s departure, *Stake Your Claim, The Ten Commandments,* and *Diagrams for Living* (based on manuscripts he left with me) have appeared under the Harper banner, and all have been highly successful publications. Fred Becker stated that as far as he knew there were only two authors whose manuscripts have become best sellers after their death: Zane Grey, writer of Western stories, and Emmet Fox.

Also since E.F.'s departure all of his works have been published in the French language,* and such is the power of his word that in translation they have become best sellers throughout the French-speaking world. In one of his lectures in New York E.F. said, "What does it matter if a man's name is Charles, or Carlos, or Carl? He is a child of God and God knows him as such." So, too, the Truth as Emmet Fox presented it is the Truth in any language.

*Librarie Astra, Paris.

Along
the Road

On our first trip west in the early thirties the plan was for Emmet Fox, Blanche, and me to drive as far as Chicago where we looked forward to seeing the World's Fair that was opened there. We left New York in high spirits, for none of us had been farther west than the Pennsylvania Poconos. As we motored through the towns and on through the Alleghenys and into Ohio, E.F. became so entranced with the United States that he decided to change his entire schedule so that we could continue right to the West Coast. This trip became the forerunner of an annual trek for the three of us that took us all over the United States, Canada, Mexico, and most of pre-Hitler Europe, all done by automobile so that we always had time for a thorough view of everything.

On this trip, when we reached Chicago, telegrams were sent canceling some speaking engagements and changing others. We were staying at the Palmer House and on our second evening there, a friend from New York looked at us in astonishment as we walked into the lobby. He invited us to dinner. Emmet Fox knew his wife from the meetings but had never met him. As we sat down to dinner, he asked, "Dr. Fox, do you mind if I have some beer with my dinner?"

E.F. laughed. "Of course not! The athletes in England all train on beer, and I think it's a lot stronger than the American product."

This was the first World's Fair Blanche and I had ever seen, and it turned out to be more than expected. In the years to come we would visit other world's fairs in San Francisco, Seattle, San Diego, Fort Worth, New York, Paris, and Brussels. Emmet Fox felt it was important to see these outstanding events, for they kept one abreast of the technological, and sometimes spiritual, achievements that were evolving.

We spent a couple of days sightseeing, and buying a lot of books. The one place that drew E.F. like a magnet was a bookshop, especially a secondhand one with long-out-of-print books. This propensity originally led him into the metaphysical movement. While browsing through second-hand bookshops in London in the early 1900s, he came across some American pamphlets on the subject. And from then on he was hooked! For this we and millions of others give thanks.

We then headed west. The roads got increasingly worse with stretches of gravel that went on for many miles. In those days there were no completely paved roads across the country no matter what route was taken. Through Kansas and Nebraska there were many miles of roads that the wheels of cars had converted into a continuing washboard that set up vibrations that made one's teeth chatter. It is amazing how the automobiles of that era stood up under the strain, not to mention the endurance of the driver and passengers. Over the prairies it seemed as though one were driving the same mile all day long, for the scenery was unchanging, but the deep abiding peace of the landscape made up for that.

In good weather, no matter where we might be, it was a daily practice for us to stop and walk into a field for a fifteen- or twenty-minute meditation, while Blanche prayed in the car. Prayer and treatment were always the paramount focus of the day. Western Union stations became our office away from home and through it we kept in touch with those who needed spiritual help. E.F. was always one to save time and keep up-to-the-minute. But that did not prevent him from being a fun person. He had a good tenor voice and liked to sing in the car. What impressed Blanche and me was that he knew the words of so many songs, popular or classic. He had a prodigious memory.

We also soon discovered that he knew interesting facts about most of the larger towns through which we were passing. I once asked him from what source his information came. He replied, "From reading the *Brooklyn Eagle* in London." I thought at first he was joking with me because I came from Brooklyn. He said that he considered the *Brooklyn Eagle* one of the outstanding newspapers of the world and had read it along with many others for years. We talked about his photographic mind and he agreed that he did have one, but, he continued, "So does everyone else, because the subconscious always remembers everything that an individual has experienced. What people have to do is to train their minds to recall information when needed." He had done just this to a remarkable degree.

In spite of the great pressure of his work he found pleasure in simple things. Once when crossing the bridge over the majestic Mississippi River, he asked me to stop the car at the state line marker. I did so and then he said, "Go forward two feet." He looked at Blanche in the back seat and laughed. "Blanche," he said, "you are still in Wisconsin, and we're in Iowa, but we'll have you out of Wisconsin in a jiffy!"

One of the places we stopped at was the Unity School which at that time had its headquarters in Kansas City, Missouri. Emmet Fox admired the teachings of Charles Fillmore, founder of Unity, and always said that he was Fillmore's spiritual son.

Emmet Fox wrote: "I look upon Charles Fillmore as being among the prophets. He has given us something that the great prophets have given us. A prophet is one who has certain contact with God in a very rare degree and gives that out to his fellowmen. He is a broadcasting station for God. We all know the great prophets in the Bible, and there have been a few outside of them. Charles Fillmore is one of the great men of this generation, although unknown as such to the world at large. The things which really are his are not the things which are so apparent on the surface. I am one of his spiritual children."

So it was a great treat and an inspiring event finally to meet Charles Fillmore, his sons Lowell and Rick, Ernest Wilson, who was then and still is a popular writer and speaker for Unity, and the entire staff of Unity School. E.F. was asked to speak at a special meeting of the workers and staff at 917 Tracy, the headquarters of Unity in Kansas City, and later to the students out at Unity Farm. And we had the pleasure of listening to Ernest Wilson.

We stayed at the Muehlebach Hotel in Kansas City but then shifted to the small hotel at Unity Farm. On one occasion we had an early meal at the cafeteria, since E.F. was to speak that evening at a large outdoor meeting. The lecture was well received and after it many people lined up to talk to him. It was late by the time we were returning to the hotel and E.F. said to us, "We had such an early meal, I feel hungry." We readily agreed we were too. "What do you say we drive in to the Muehlebach to have a bite!" Off we went.

When we returned to the hotel at Unity Farm, everything was very quiet with not a soul around. Our rooms were on the second floor, and as we made our way up the dimly lighted stairway E.F. whispered, "We'd better remove our shoes so as not to wake anyone." When we reached the top, E.F. dropped one of his shoes and it went bouncing down the stairs. He whispered to us with a chuckle, "Your sins will always find you out." We never learned whether or not our sins were found out, for we never heard anything about the matter.

On another evening we were sitting on the veranda in front of the cafeteria, sipping black cows (a delicious mixture of root beer and vanilla ice cream) with Charles Fillmore and a number of others. It was very hot, and someone mentioned how annoying the flies were, to which Charles Fillmore in his keen sense of humor responded, "There may be a few flies around here but there are no flies on Jesus." With its beauty and spiritual ambiance, Unity was a fun place to be.

This also happened with the kinship felt for the Divine Science Church co-founded by Nona Brooks and located in Denver, Colorado. If Charles Fillmore was E.F.'s spiritual father, Nona Brooks was surely his spiritual mother. He adored her and so did we. When Blanche and I first met Nona Brooks early one morning in a hotel in Omaha, Nebraska, Blanche wrote in her diary: "She is one of the most charming persons I have ever met. I could listen to her talk all day, she is so interesting." We met in the lobby. Nona was wearing a little hat and with his English reserve, E.F. tilted it back and kissed her forehead. She blushed clear up to her temples! We spent the day with Nona; she was on her way East and we were headed West.

There was prolonged and ravaging drought in the Middle West and we saw the evidence of it everywhere: parched land, dead cattle in the fields, and people leaving their dust-bowl farms in rickety cars with all their meager possessions in the hope of finding a "better pasture" in California. On one occasion the dust blowing across the road was so severe that we had to stop the car. E.F. said, "This is a good time to pray for rain." We stayed there perhaps twenty minutes; the dust storm subsided, and we continued on. But in a half hour we had to stop again. There was so much rain coming down that we could not see the road. We sat there giving thanks as probably many other people were doing, for the storm had broken the long drought.

The next afternoon as we drove over the brow of a small hill, we were given our first view of the geological backbone of the country, the blue and gold grandeur of the Rockies, stretched across the horizon. We got out of the car and thanked God for bringing us to that memorable place.

We reached Denver a day or so later and had our first face-to-face introduction to all the folks at the First Divine Science Church, and at the Colorado Divine Science College, the headquarters for the movement. It was there in 1932 that Emmet Fox gave a lecture on "The Historical Destiny of the United States—The Mystery of the American Money," which was later published by Harper & Brothers. As early as 1938 some of the predictions he made in that lecture had already come true.

As the years passed we made many visits to Denver, during which E.F. lectured and all of us had a grand time. We were truly introduced to the hospitality of the west. Once we were taken to a dinner gathering at Heidi's Chalet.

Everyone was there, people we would know and love in the ensuing years. Heidi's looked as if it had been carried by magic carpet from Switzerland and put down in a similar setting in the Rocky Mountains. Other places we visited were Red Rock Park and the Garden of the Gods. We got to know famous names and places of the west such as Central City and its small but famous Opera House of the gold rush days where Jenny Lind and other noted singers had sung. There, too, George Rasely, who was the soloist at our Sunday services in New York, had sung "The Bartered Bride."

On one trip to Colorado Springs E.F. started saying early on, "Pike's Peak or bust!" just as the early pioneers used to. He was becoming more American every mile of the way. Eventually we started up the long rough trail to the top of the peak. E.F. was overjoyed and kept repeating "Pike's Peak or bust!"—at a height of 14,000 feet. The farther up we climbed the harder it was for the car to breathe. In a jovial mood E.F. said, "We ought to nickname this Ford 'Chamois,' because it gets us every place we want to go." From then on we would have a new "Chamois" each year, clocking about 30,000 miles annually. We did not know at that time that Henry Ford would eventually become interested in Emmet Fox's books and request them from our New York office.

But on this trip our "Chamois" was not exactly bounding from peak to peak, but rather from rock to rock. It was a rough road, and oxygen was getting thin for "Chamois" and for us. At one point I got out and adjusted the carburetor, which was easy to do with the simple mechanisms of the early cars. "Chamois" did better after that, and we finally reached the parking place not far from the top, as E.F. continued his shouts of "Pike's Peak or bust!"

As I stopped the car, he bounded out the door to be the

first to the top—but he had not reckoned with the altitude. He had gone but a short distance when he was completely out of breath and had to lay on the road. When he regained his breath and his humor, he said, "The early pioneers surely must have been a hardy lot."

One of our trips took us to Nevada where we saw old mining towns, some of which were ghost towns with only the shells of buildings still standing. We stopped for lunch in Tonopah. There was only one hotel, and as we parked the car we saw a woman coming out of what was apparently the bar, carrying a large can of beer. E.F. laughed and said, "Just like the pubs in England. There they come out a side door with a pint under their shawl." But the "pint" in Tonopah looked more like two quarts.

Behind the hotel was quite a hill that seemed to rise abruptly and looked as if it might slide down and engulf the whole building at any moment. We went into the restaurant that boasted "Home Cooking" on its windows, and E.F. remarked, "I'm always wary of home cooking along the road." And from experience we agreed with him.

The proprietor, like most westerners, was friendly and talkative. He handed us a weather-beaten menu and asked, "Where are you folks from?"

"New York," we answered.

"Could have told you were tenderfeet the minute you walked in the door."

Eventually the meal was served. He came over again. "What business are you in?"

"I'm a clergyman," E.F. answered.

"Oh, you're one of those preacher fellows. Well, reverend, did you see that mountain behind the hotel?"

Winking at us, E.F. replied, "One could hardly miss it!"

"Well, reverend, every day I look at that mountain, and

as the Bible says, I say to it, 'Be you removed and cast into the sea.' I been doin' it for a good many years, and it hasn't moved yet." He spoke it like a challenge, as if to say, "You're a preacher; do something about it."

We left the hotel with the hill still standing there—and a little later wished we had left the meal there too.

We spent that night in the little mining town of Ely whose local bar had a small gambling casino. After dinner at the hotel E.F., who always wanted to see everything, said facetiously, "Let's be real daring and go in and have a look."

There was a rough-type crowd inside but we did not falter and walked boldly, we thought, up to the bar. It seemed as if every face turned toward us but we took courage when we saw a young woman tending bar. We fumbled over what to order, E.F. and Blanche finally settling for coffee, and I, hoping to save face, ordered a beer. The beer came quickly but the coffee had to be made. When Blanche asked for milk for it, the barmaid said, "Honey, I bet you're getting a big kick out of this. I know I did when I first went into a bar down in Mexicali." And then she added, "We don't have any milk. We only use coffee to sober up some of our customers."

In a day or two we arrived at the California border. Driving into California was like crossing the frontier into a foreign country. Border guards examined the luggage and the car, searching for fruits and vegetables carrying beetles or some other agricultural pest. They also watched for other things. For several years, the so-called Okies, farmers from the dust bowls of Oklahoma and other states, headed for California to sell anything they had to get themselves solvent again.

With his penchant for collecting books E.F. had about fifty or sixty of them in the car. The inspector eyed the books and asked, "Mister, what are you going to do with all them thar books?"

E.F. replied, "I'm going to read them."

"Are you sure you ain't goin' to sell them in California? What business are you in?"

"I'm a clergyman."

"Oh," said the inspector, "you're a reverend. Well, I guess it's all right." And he passed us through. This happened with variations almost every time we crossed into California.

Later in the afternoon we decided to stop at the first town we came to. It was hot as the town was close to the desert, and few people were around. We asked a chap where the best hotel in town was. He thought a minute and then said, "Well, there are two hotels in town, small ones, and no matter which one you pick, you'll wish you had picked the other." There was no air conditioning in those days and so a fan blowing hot air around the room was the only means of gaining some relief. But the next afternoon near the bottom of Death Valley we were to find a very ingenious cooling device.

Death Valley was more wonderful than we had anticipated. The scenery was absolutely stupendous with fantastic formations and colors. As we motored deeper and deeper into it, mirages appeared from time to time. Lakes and bodies of water that really did not exist were the phenomenon of nature that caused the death of so many early pioneers who were lured out to them as they sought water for themselves and their livestock. Yet in spite of this tragic history the scene was very beautiful.

Warning signs cautioned travelers not to stray from the main roads that were patroled, and not to leave the car in case of a breakdown. The dry heat was very deceptive. One never felt any perspiration because it dried off so quickly.

About halfway down we stopped at the famous Zabry-skie Point where we could see the deepest and highest places in the United States simultaneously. E.F. said, "I read about this and saw pictures of it and the 20-Mule Borax Team in England, but this far surpasses my imagination." Far below us the salt flats shimmered in the hot sun—the second deepest place on earth—and towering in the distance was the snowcapped Mt. Whitney, the highest point.

Later that afternoon as we wound our way down toward the bottom of Death Valley, our big surprise was an oasis—a date palm ranch with the very believable name in that 120° temperature of Furnace Creek Ranch. Years later in the Middle East we were to have a similar experience, but this was our first contact with fresh dates on growing palm trees. Here at Furnace Creek Ranch they had overnight accommodations for tenderfeet from the East. E.F. was so entranced that he said, "Let's spend the night here," although it was then only 3 P.M. With the temperature so high outside we were amazed to find that inside the cabins the temperature was only 80°. Air conditioning was achieved by allowing water to drip through a box of straw set in the window and the evaporating power of the dry heat outside cooled the air that came into the cabin. We would spend a very comfortable night.

The long afternoon and evening were not wasted. It was often in times like this that E.F. did some of his best writing, and we worked together on a new booklet scheduled to come out in the fall.

A few years later when we revisited Death Valley, E.F. had a hunch that we ought to drive some miles away through the Valley and meet Death Valley Scotty. While in England E.F. had heard of Scotty and his exploits and wanted to see the man himself if possible. So off we went, and after driving for awhile in heat and dust we got very thirsty. A sign on the road, "Stove Pipe Wells," only served to confirm our thirst, and we did not stop to investigate. When, after a couple of hours more, there was still no sign of habitation, E.F. said, "I think this situation calls for spiritual treatment." Not too long after treating, we came upon a small roadside shack with a crude sign, "Restaurant—Home Cooking." Another "Home Cooking" sign! E.F. laughed and said, "I guess it's part of our karma, but it certainly is better than nothing." We were more thirsty than hungry. We found we had a choice of warm soda pop, warm beer, warm milk, or cool water. The owner was an old prospector who had finally settled down and had a cow grazing in what grass could be found among the cactus. We ordered fried egg sandwiches and cool water which came from a spring nearby.

This old sourdough told us he had prospected for gold for many years, hoping to strike it rich like Scotty, but his gleanings had been meager and he finally gave it up. He also acknowledged that his restaurant was not doing too well either, mostly because there were not too many travelers out that way.

Death Valley Scotty was believed to have a secret gold mine, and every so often he would go up into the hills to sustain that impression. He had a reputation for making unusual and expensive gestures. He hired a special train from the Atchison, Topeka and Santa Fe Railroad to set the fastest run from Los Angeles to Chicago. He also built "Scotty's Castle," a two-million-dollar Moorish castle in Grapevine Canyon which the famous architect Frank Lloyd Wright designed.

As we approached it, the castle seemed like a mirage from The Arabian Nights tales, too beautiful and grand to be believed, flanked by tall palm trees and a swimming pool. All this in the middle of the desert! The building was of Italian marble, the kitchen and bathrooms were of Spanish tiles, the music room had a grand piano, and the dining room had crystal chandeliers.

We reached the entrance and rang the door chimes. E.F. identified himself to the man servant, and said he would like to see Mr. Scott. (E.F.'s English reserve had not yet been completely dissipated.) The man asked us to please wait. In minutes Scotty himself came out to greet us. It turned out that Scotty had read *The Sermon on the Mount* and was very glad to meet the author in person. We were invited to dinner and to spend the night there.

We had a fine meal served in sumptuous surroundings, and then as often happens at good parties, the four of us retired to the kitchen, the Spanish tiles on the walls giving it great beauty. Scotty, wearing his ten-gallon and boots, sat in a corner with his feet up on a chair, chewing tobacco. There was a spitoon nearby, and Scotty seldom missed it. Then he told us stories of his early hard times at gold prospecting, and it was good to hear the tales from the man himself.

E.F. asked, "Scotty"—it had become Scotty now—"what do you do when you have a real problem?"

"Well, reverend, I get by myself with a gallon of bootleg gin, and I think it out." And then he laughed and said, "I'm not a religious man, but I pray too."

Many people know now a secret that was well kept for a long time: Scotty did strike it very rich. Albert M. Johnson of Chicago, chairman of the National Life Insurance Company, and a man of considerable wealth, was very ill with tuberculosis. Scotty coaxed him out to the dry desert climate where he lived in Scotty's shack. Johnson was healed and as a result he financed Scotty in all his unusual exploits.

MEXICO

In 1935 we made our first trip to Mexico, and I mention the year because life there was a lot more primitive in those days. We had to be vaccinated, and although it was a nuisance, we saw the wisdom of this when we were in Mexico and passed some houses with notices stating "Viruela" (smallpox).

Emmet Fox was always full of fun on these trips. In Gettysburg, Pennsylvania, he bought Pluto the Pup as a mascot, and a box of Barbara Fritchie candy as a patriotic gesture.

Following the Sky Line Drive, one of the most beautiful roads in the eastern United States, we stayed overnight at the Stonewall Jackson Hotel in Staunton, Virginia. The next morning E.F. came down to breakfast laughing heartily. As with ourselves, a waiter had come to his room with small cups of black coffee and the greeting, "Good morning, would you care for an 'eye-opener.' " E.F. slyly remarked to us, "I wonder if they serve that to all the ministers!"

The next day we stopped for lunch at the Nu-Wray Hotel in Burnsville, North Carolina, where we joined thirty or forty people at a long table that was covered with platters of delectable food. We never saw so much at one table anywhere else, and E.F. said, "It's no use my telling people in England about it. They would never believe it."

We stayed in the dining room so long that we missed the time for the one-way road up Mt. Mitchell, the highest peak in the Appalachian chain; but with treatment the sympathetic guard let us through and we made the ascent. Magnificent views all around . . . Later, going through the Smoky Mountains, we were thrilled to see Cherokee Indians camped along the road. E.F. said jokingly, "I didn't expect to find Indians so close to 'home,' " and then added, "In England there are some people, especially the youngsters, who have an idea that Indians are galloping around Broadway [New York]."

The next day we stopped in Little Rock, Arkansas, which years later was to hit the headlines over conflict with school integration programs. We found it a peaceful and interesting capital city. Three days later we were in San Antonio where we each picked up a Tourist Card, but since E.F. still held "foreigner" status, he had to have his picture taken.

Finally we were at the border in Laredo, Texas, and drove down what is probably one of the longest stretches of straight road, to Monterrey. We stayed at the Colonial Hotel which was situated on a park, and in the evening we saw an interesting sight. Girls with their chaperones walked in a large circle under the trees, and the boys walked in the other direction. There was much whispering going on, which the Mexicans call "bisbiseo," and it carried a quiet musical effect. Eventually some of the girls and boys went off in pairs under the discreetly watchful eyes of the chaperones. E.F. commented, "This is not at all like London or New York but in Latin countries there is a tendency to protect their girls more. This is boy-meets-girl, Mexican style."

We had intended leaving the next morning but word came that because of torrential rains, the road toward Mexico City was impassable. We made good use of the time and visited a wonderful fruit market. But we had been warned not to eat any raw fruit. We went on to the Bishop's Palace on a hill outside the town. It had been occupied by only one bishop back in the 1800s but the building and the surrounding scenery were still impressive.

In the afternoon we went to beautifully scenic Chipinque Mountain. The three of us took a burro ride through Huastic Canyon. We thought it a little ridiculous for adults to be riding such small animals, but later as we got farther into Mexico we found this was the usual means of travel as it had been in Jesus' time, so we were rather thrilled, after all, to resemble a Bible picture. We took pictures of each other and everything went well until the guide, tired of walking over the rough ground, jumped on the donkey E.F. was riding. E.F. thought that was too much for the animal, so we returned to our car pleased but feeling that burros cannot match the soft cushions of an automobile. That evening we went to the casino to watch gambling Mexican style, which turned out to be much like casinos of every style with most people losing and a few gaining money.

The next day the rains stopped and we were able to continue. For two days we drove south, passing lush vegetation fields, sugar plantations, and thatched Indian huts. We headed toward a town called Tomazunchale which we nicknamed Thomas an' Charlie. We were surprised to discover that we had to cross, via barges, three fast-flowing rivers in order to get there. Each barge held two cars and was attached to a cable strung across the river. The ferrymen maneuvered the barge so that the pressure of the fast-flowing water propelled it across the river. Eleven years later when we made another trip to Mexico City, fine bridges spanned the rivers. We were somewhat disappointed, however, that tourism had brought so many other changes. Little towns had become big ones, hotels were larger, Coca Cola stands and the other signs of commercialism were everywhere.

We reached Tomazunchale after dark. In all these towns boys wanted to act as guides whether there was anything to see or not. And since cars in those days had running boards, there was no escape. The only way to solve the problem was to select one of them. So we chose our guide and went to the Hotel Vega, but because of the late hour there was "no room in the inn" for Emmet Fox. He was always concerned that we should have the best, so we had our room there and he stayed close by with a Mexican family.

At that time the Pan-American Highway was not completed, and Tomazunchale was the starting point for the climb along a precipitous road that reached an elevation of 8,300 feet from which it then dropped into Mexico City whose altitude is 7,400 feet, one of the highest in the world. The hotelkeeper advised us to be on our way by 6 A.M. as the road would be closed at noon.

So we started out bright and early. We were only sixteen miles away from Tomazunchale, climbing steadily on the muddy road, when we were stopped by a line of ten cars. Eventually there were forty more behind us, cars with members of the International Lions Club who were holding a convention in Mexico City. But that was the saving grace—there were always angels on our shoulders. Because of the convention the Mexican Government had ordered the engineers to make the road passable. But a week before, torrential rains had caused a landslide at this particular point, completely cutting off further access. The engineers, who had been using a steam shovel to dig the road out again, had the task almost completed the night before we arrived. They had left the steam shovel standing in the middle of the narrow road as there was no other place for it. However, nature played a trick and a cloudburst that night had caused another landslide, burying the steam shovel. Gangs of workmen were trying to dig a path *over* the steam shovel, for there was no way around it.

We sat there in the car treating and praying for them as well as for all of us involved. Young boys came up from the villages and E.F. gave them a few pesos. Pretty soon by some form of "telepathy" there were dozens of boys coming to the car for a handout while the foremen of the job tried shooing them away. Natives from the valleys arrived with warm soda pop and warm beer, and E.F. bought drinks for the workmen. It took seven hours in intense heat but the workmen never stopped. E.F. observed, "There is no one in England or America who would work like this." We had great admiration for the Mexicans.

Finally the first attempt to get the cars over the steam shovel began. We continued treating as the first car was pulled with ropes by twenty-five or thirty men while the driver did his best to assist with the engine. Sometimes cars got stuck and the workmen crawled underneath to free them, or a group of them would lift the car bodily. When our turn came I insisted that Blanche and E.F. get out and walk. In the end we made it and headed for a town with the strange name of Ixmiquilpan.

A surprise was waiting for us there. It was late and quite dark and we were besieged by the usual guides. We selected one young boy and he led us down a pitch-black street. We kept saying, "Hotel, hotel," and he kept replying, "No, *mizzizzoney, mizzizzoney.*" When we finally reached what looked like a hotel, we learned that once again there were no rooms. The hotelkeeper also said, "*Mizzizzoney.* Muchacho take you."

There was nothing else to do but follow our guide's directions down a street to a big iron gate. He jumped off the running board, ran over to the adobe wall, and pulled a rope. We heard a bell clanking way in the distance. It took so long for anyone to answer that Blanche and I felt sure we were wasting our time, but E.F. persisted: "Let us just know that God is working in this situation and taking care of us."

Soon an old man bent over like the hunchback of Notre

Dame came to the gate with a lantern. Our guide rattled off a lot of Spanish and the man disappeared in the darkness. Another wait and then a vision of loveliness in a flowing white gown appeared, carrying a lantern. She spoke to us in English and asked how many in our party. I said, "Three." She asked if there were a woman with us, and when I answered, "Yes, my wife," she said, "Let her come with me. *Mrs. Honey* would like to talk to her." Blanche and the lady went off into the darkness. They were soon back with an invitation from Mrs. Honey for us to spend the night in her villa. Outside blackness; inside magnificence.

When Miss Gravelly, who had met us at the gate, realized it was Emmet Fox (she had read some of his booklets) she was eager to talk to him. We were introduced to Mrs. Honey who was having a bout with malaria. After dinner Emmet Fox spent several hours with them. And in the morning Mrs. Honey was well enough to have breakfast with us. Before we parted, she said she was eager to have us meet her sons, who were in the banking business in Mexico City. It turned out that the appointment could not be arranged.

As we neared Mexico City later that day, we had our first view of Popocatepetl and its sister volcano with the unpronounceable name of Ixtacihuatl—The Sleeping Woman. Once again the hotels were filled up, but E.F. was not disturbed. He said, "Let's treat as we ride along the streets." Following the flow of traffic, we turned a corner, and there in front of us was a sign: Hotel Regis. E.F. said immediately, "We'll find rooms there." We did—a beautiful penthouse apartment overlooking the whole city.

We found Mexico City a beautiful town, not unlike Paris. There was so much to see and do that we hardly knew where to begin. But E.F., always interested in Biblical and occult symbolism, was soon at the museum researching the omen that had first led the Aztecs to found this city in the early fourteenth century.

The Aztec priests had said they were to establish their city, Tenochtitlan, at a place where they found an eagle perched on a cactus, clutching a snake in its beak. These have become part of the Mexican symbolism. In Egyptian symbolism a snake is also used. The ankh on the forehead of the sphinx is an adder (representing Spirit).* The eagle is a symbol of spiritual as well as material victory. The Spirit always subdues the lower nature, represented by a snake which, when finally spiritualized, no longer slithers through the grass to bite the heel of man (his vulnerable spot) but takes its tail in its mouth, evolving into the symbol of eternity.

We found many Mexicans of Aztec and Mayan stock and their works so resembled that of the Egyptians that E.F. felt both must have been part of the Atlantean civilization. We visited the great Pyramids of the Sun and of the Moon, the Pyramid of the Sun being larger than the Pyramid at Gizeh in Cairo. Its stones are smaller but its passages and burial vaults are similar. There is one difference, however, between the two. It is believed that these pyramids in Mexico were used for human sacrifice. From the Pyramid of the Sun to the Pyramid of the Moon lies the Avenue of the Dead. The lower sides of the structures often are decorated with grotesque figures. The builders of the pyramids in Mexico apparently had a knowledge of astronomy and calculated time on a fairly accurate calendar.

We also visited a number of the public buildings, all beautifully laid out but slowly sinking (at least at that time) because Mexico City is largely built on swampland

*See *Diagrams for Living*, pp. 73 and 74.

and natural drainage has affected building foundations. Yet this has also been a blessing. The occasional earthquakes in the area are not nearly so severe as they otherwise would be. While we were in Mexico City, there were a couple of tremors but we were not unduly alarmed. E.F. commented, "Underneath are the Everlasting Arms."

Churches and cathedrals are everywhere in Mexico. In the town of Puebla we entered a church lavishly decorated with gold, and E.F. spotted a soldier with a gun hidden behind one of the pillars. He whispered to us, "They aren't taking any chances with us gringos." In Cholula it is said there are 365 churches and chapels, one for every day of the year. We did not stop to count them! Some were built on top of the ruins of more ancient places of worship. We could not help but observe the contrasting poverty of many of the inhabitants.

On our way to Nevada de Toluca, a volcano with two lakes on top, we had to go up through a pass at 10,000 feet. The road was the same kind of gooey mud we had encountered on the Pan-American Highway, and we got stuck in a huge puddle that spanned the road. More prayer work had to be done. We had seen very few cars but again E.F. said, "Well, we treated before coming on this trip, and God is providing a way." As a matter of fact, prayer was always a prerequisite. It was not long before a bus came from the opposite direction loaded with men hanging on all sides of it. When they saw our plight, about twenty of them came wading through the mud and pushed our car onto dry ground. E.F. freely distributed pesos, and others from the bus joined their fellow travelers' good fortune. For us it was really a godsend. This was the kind of giving we always saw Mexicans offering.

Before leaving Mexico we took a boat ride among the floating gardens of Xochimilco. I say *boat* ride, but it was more like a small barge completely decorated with a canopy and flowers. Other small boats came alongside with photographers, and natives selling trinkets, sweet cakes, and drinks. The brightly colored soda pop was everywhere. E.F. joined in the fun and we had pictures taken.

We wanted to go across Mexico to Acapulco, which then was just a small fishing village on the Pacific Ocean, but our time was running out and we had to head north. We did manage to see a bullfight before leaving. The fanfare and crowd response was interesting, but after seeing a couple of bulls slain, we had had enough and left. Its singular good, we thought, was the distribution of meat to the poor.

We found that on the way back to the border the road was somewhat improved. (Even so, we had to get four new tires in Texas.) Our stop for the night was in the little town of Jacala where we met a British mining engineer by the name of Tom Simpson who got us rooms in a small hotel. Having had a touch of dysentery in Mexico City, we took no chances with our diet and ordered boiled eggs and tea for dinner. E.F. was a confirmed tea drinker so Blanche and I usually ordered tea also. He said facetiously that he only drank coffee to make the next cup of tea taste better.

All through the U.S. and Canada E.F. would try to teach waiters and waitresses how to make tea. He abhorred a small teapot of hot water with the tea bag wrapped around the neck of the pot or lying on the saucer. He would send it back, patiently explaining that the tea bag must be put in the pot first and boiling water poured over it. One afternoon, when crossing Lake Michigan—a six-hour trip by boat—we ordered our usual tea. When the steward, a rather burly fellow, brought it in a very small pot, E.F. asked for some more very hot water. We waited so long, the tea became lukewarm, and when the steward finally reappeared with a pitcher of hot water big enough to bathe with, he explained it was boiled "special." After a couple of years of this, E.F. gave in and said, "I had better stick to metaphysics."

But this time in Mexico we had a different problem. The tea was hot, as E.F. liked it, but its color was that of pale lemonade and it certainly did not smell or taste like tea. Using my best Spanish (while E.F. laughed at my struggling with the language), I said to the waitress, "Mas te!" (more tea). She took the pot of tea and when she returned, it was slightly yellower. This went on several times until she shrugged her shoulders and walked away. We found out later what the trouble was. They had no real tea but boiled the leaves from the orange tree in the garden.

That night we slept on the hardest beds we had ever had.

The next morning Tom Simpson invited us to his home for breakfast and it more than made up for the lack of the evening before. He had the table laid out with silver and crystal and beautiful English china, and a delicious English breakfast.

We finally reached Laredo, Texas, several days later.

Yet that was not the end of Mexico for us. The next year, returning from the West Coast, we took a southern route across the U.S., crossing over the border several times. One of the towns was Mexicali. The barmaid we had met a year earlier at the gambling casino in Ely, Nevada, said she had gained her experience in that "wide open" town. Now we understood exactly what she had meant.

We stayed in El Paso overnight and that evening visited the town of Juarez across the border. Its biggest attraction was its prison. It was an open-air affair with high walls, no

roof, and immense iron gates that seemed more open than
shut. Although we felt a little uneasy when the gates first
closed behind us, the guide whispered in broken English,
"Don't be afraid. Nothing will happen."

Some prisoners were in for minor infractions, others
more serious, as a woman who was doing a life sentence for
murdering her husband. The guide said, "She speaks English." E.F. was eager to talk to her. The guide went over
to where she was lying on a cot and gave her a nudge, but
no response. He did this a couple of times, and the
only answer was some mumbled Spanish and she rolled
over. E.F., with his humor, said, "After all, if she is going
to be here the rest of her life, she's not going to have her
sleep disturbed by tourists." Some prisoners carved letter
openers from bull horns, which under the circumstances
seemed like lethal weapons. We bought a number of these
and E.F. turned to us and said, "Maybe we would be safer
if we bought them all up!"

EUROPE

Although Emmet Fox traveled frequently to Europe, it
was not until 1937 that we accompanied him. After a very
delightful crossing we disembarked from the *S.S. Beren-
garia* at Cherbourg, France, on a very hot day. We stopped
in a cafe for a bottle of Cidre Bouché. E.F. commented it
tasted better than anything made in England and we
added, "or in the U.S." Normandie is noted for its excellent cider, both sweet and hard. It was our favorite drink
on the way to Paris, and in Paris at Fouquet's it was served
like champagne in a bucket.

We spent our first night at the Hotel Angleterre in
Caen,* and Blanche and I were amazed to hear E.F. rattle

---

*See chapter, "*The Psychic-Spiritual Side.*

off in French to the proprietress who complimented him: "Monsieur, you speak such good French." Then thinking that we did too, she turned to Blanche and said, "Vous êtes tres jolie!" She repeated it several times while Blanche smiled indulgently, and then turned to E.F. for translation. He was blushing a bit as he said, "She says you are very pretty." And then Blanche blushed too. This was our introduction to the hospitality of France.

E.F. delighted in visiting the cathedrals, museums, and galleries of Europe. So the next morning we went to the famous cathedral at Lisieux, the shrine of the Little Flower. With E.F.'s expert guidance Europe became not only the Grand Tour but it was also a postgraduate course in beaux-arts, architecture, and history spiced with political and religious intrigue. His knowledge was absolutely astounding and he could easily have rewritten *Baedeker's Guide*, the traveler's Bible in those days.

On the way to Paris we had a brief look at the cathedral in Rouen, and also the market place. Lunch at one of the fine restaurants there gave us our first taste of some of the delicious French specialties of the region. Then we headed for the Grand Hotel in Paris of which E.F. was especially fond as his mother and father honeymooned there. There was "no room in the inn," again, but the hotel graciously arranged reservations for us at the Chateau Frontenac, which was to be our home in Paris not only then but also in 1938, 1950, and 1951, and from which E.F. would ultimately take his final departure.

Our sightseeing included the Louvre, especially the Mona Lisa, the Tuilleries, and Notre Dame Cathedral. Blanche and I wanted to see the gargoyles and E.F. said, "I've seen them before but you must not miss them." So we climbed up while he sat in the cathedral and did some spiritual treatment.

In our sightseeing, one of the things Blanche and I did not expect was a visit to a cemetery. It was Père Lachaise, one of the famous cemeteries of Europe where the list of persons buried there reads like a Who's Who of the theater, music, history, and the arts. We visited a number of graves: Sarah Bernhardt, Victor Hugo, Bizet, and Verdi of whose music E.F. was especially fond. Each site received a blessing as we passed. This was to be, fourteen years later, the place where Emmet Fox's ashes reposed for a month before being brought back to America on his favorite ship, the *Ile de France*. At the time of our visit to Père Lachaise, E.F. said, "All good Englishmen and Americans come to Paris to die." How prophetic he was!

Paris has so many excellent restaurants with "out-of-this-world" food that one can only mention one's favorites. Emmet Fox had his own too. Occasionally we dined at Maxim's made famous by Toulouse Lautrec, where E.F. always insisted upon a little footstool for Blanche. Privately she told me she did not need one but she liked the "cute" idea.

As a steady favorite E.F. liked to have lunch at Fouquet's on the Champs Élysées where more often than not we had filet of sole and a bottle of Sylvaner. Evenings found us at La Coupole in Montparnasse. Le Dome was next door and was the famous rendezvous for Ernest Hemingway, the F. Scott Fitzgeralds, and others of the artistic and literary crowd. (Years later we were to meet Ernest Hemingway when he was "master of ceremonies" at the gala on the *S.S. Flandre* where Blanche was the principal singer.)

At Fouquet's E.F. was especially interested in a young busboy, often slipping him money gifts. The boy was probably fourteen or fifteen but very enterprising and anxious to do a good job. He wore a tailed coat that was ill-

fitting and shoes much too large. After E.F. got friendly
with him, the boy said that the clothes belonged to his
father who had been a waiter. E.F. turned to us: "That's
the way in Europe. The boys follow in their father's foot-
steps. If he keeps working the way he does, he'll probably
be head waiter some day. But how much better it is in
America, where a boy has the opportunity to be whatever
he fits himself for." (Europe was that way in those years, a
situation that would change after World War II. Devastat-
ing as it was, the war also had constructive effects. It al-
tered the attitudes of people, and today the system in
Europe is much closer to the American idea of equal opportunity for everyone.)

E.F. wanted Blanche and me to see everything we could
in Paris. He knew Paris as well as he did London. So we
experienced all facets of Parisian life from the exalted to
the ordinary, from hearing a mass at the Madeleine to
watching the dancers in an apache nightclub where the
men wore their berets and colorful garb while dancing
with the women. One evening we went to a restaurant in
the Montmartre section. At the top of the Butte there is
the famous Sacré Coeur cathedral with its gleaming white
domes overlooking all of Paris—a truly magnificent view
night or day. On this particular occasion the restaurant
we stopped at was a gay place with music and dancing.
A smart-looking young man approached, bowed, and asked
E.F. in French for permission to dance with his daughter.
We all laughed and the young man became embarrassed.
E.F. explained the circumstances; the fellow looked at me
and gracefully withdrew. E.F. told us that his French was
flavored with a German accent.

In due course we started on our trip. Both Hitler and
Mussolini were in power, but as Americans we had no
trouble crossing any of the borders. In one case we crossed

through a small part of Germany without passports. The German border guards spoke no English, but they obligingly called a young woman from a nearby house, who spoke both German and French. So we had a double translation of English to French to German, E.F. acting as translator from English to French. The border guards relished the situation and gave us a temporary visa.

Inadvertently Mussolini helped us. His government placed certain restrictions on wages and prices, and as a result we had to buy hotel coupons ahead of time. This worked to our advantage. E.F. had only one rule in selecting hotels—the best. So all we had to do was work out our travel schedule in advance, purchase our hotel coupons, and reservations were automatically made. Whether it was Rome, Florence, Siena, or Venice, we had the best.

The first place E.F. wanted to visit in Rome was St. Peter's. At its entrance the Swiss Guards stopped Blanche because she was wearing a dress with short sleeves. She had already covered her head with a veil. We took a coat from the car, and she had to walk around wearing it in the heat. There were small groups of visitors inside with guides explaining all the marvels, but with our own special guide, E.F. himself, we soon had a crowd of English and Americans around us. His magnetism had taken over. As we left St. Peter's, suddenly we heard some voices shouting, "Dr. Fox! Dr. Fox!" They were people from New York who had often attended meetings. They insisted that we join them for dinner at the famous Alfredo's where spaghetti is a ritual as well as a culinary delight. Recognition of Emmet Fox was just as common in sophisticated Europe as it was in the "wilds" of America.

The next day we visited the catacombs of Rome where the early Christians hid to escape the Roman authorities. E.F. pointed out the fish symbols inscribed on the walls that were the early insignia of the Christians before the cross. We followed our Roman guide carefully through the dimly lit labyrinth, as he cautioned, perhaps with tongue in cheek, that in the past there were people who had never been found—and we could believe him.

One evening we went to an outdoor opera in the beautiful ruins near the Colisseum. It was a moonlit night, and with the towering columns around us, a delightful setting. E.F. managed to get aisle seats. The orchestra started the familiar notes of *La Traviata*, when suddenly the music stopped and we heard applause and cheering in the distance. Mussolini passed beside us while people whistled and cheered with utter freedom much like that of an American audience. E.F. said to us, "This is not what we have been reading in the newspapers."

In Florence we toured the famous museums and cathedral. E.F. never tired. He was as eager as a college student. The sun was beginning to set when we reached the famous Ponte Vecchio, and a golden glow was reflected on the River Arno. There was a space between the shops in the middle of the bridge where we could look out and it was there that E.F. asked Blanche to sing the famous Italian aria, "O Mio Bambino." Blanche demurred, but E.F. insisted. Finally, she began to sing sotto voce, and eventually quite a crowd gathered, and E.F. enjoyed his new role of impressario. People applauded at the end and threw coins. E.F. said jokingly, "Maybe we ought to continue this and we could pay our passage around Europe."

In Siena with its zebra-striped cathedral, it was E.F.'s turn to be barred from entering. The weather was very hot and he had left his coat in the car, which was parked some distance away. Rather than retrieve it, he laughed and used the sour grapes excuse of "not wanting to see it anyway."

We arrived by gondola at the landing dock of the Grand Hotel in Venice to discover thirty or forty suitcases loaded on it. These belonged to the Duke and Duchess of Windsor who presently appeared and boarded their private motor launch. The delight was that we got their suite with our hotel coupons! We learned one important fact about Venice: one had to wear comfortable shoes. Picturesque as the canals are, there are of necessity many small vaulted bridges with steps going up and down. E.F. said he could understand, although he did not agree with what U.S. Grant declared of Venice, that it would really be a great city if they would fill in the canals and make decent streets out of them. E.F. added, "Typical American practicality—but not much romance."

We did a lot of traveling around Venice by gondola, especially in the evening after dinner. At that time there was not so much motor boat traffic as there is today. The gondolas would gather around a lighted platform floating in the Grand Canal opposite the Doges Palace in St. Mark's Square. Singers and musicians sat on the platform, and a tenor never failed to sing "O Sole Mio" at least once during the evening. E.F. loved to sing and joined with the others. He had a pleasant tenor voice himself and once he coaxed Blanche into a duet that ended in applause and shouts of "Bravo! Bravo!"

E.F. had two favorite places in Venice: the tall column with the winged lion on top at the water's edge in St. Mark's Square, and the balustrade with the four bronze horses of the Apocalypse in front of the magnificent Basilica of St. Mark. He was fascinated with these and explained that their symbolism illustrated how the savants of the ages, as far back as prehistoric times, had transmitted "inner" teaching.

Upon leaving Venice it was E.F.'s desire, for reasons of

his own, to visit Dr. Carl Jung in Switzerland on July 30, E.F.'s birthday. However, we miscalculated the time needed to get through the Alpine passes as we could not resist viewing at length all the beauty around us. We reached Zurich on July 31, and E.F. spent the afternoon with Dr. Jung. When they parted each had an increased admiration for the work the other was doing.

On the way to Montreux, we climbed by car to the town of Leysin, tucked away in the mountains where the Société des Etablisements Héliotherapiques was located. E.F. wanted a firsthand look at the great work Dr. A. Rollier, the founder, was doing through heliotherapy in the healing of tuberculosis of the bone in children, and of the lungs in adults. It was a thrilling experience. E.F. asked Dr. Rollier how he had started his work. Dr. Rollier answered that it began almost by accident but he felt it was providential. Some years before, his dog suffered a deep gash in its leg and the doctor bandaged it. It was not long, however, before the dog had it off. The doctor put another bandage on, tied more securely, but within half an hour the dog had it off. Dr. Rollier, curious as to how the dog accomplished this, bandaged the leg again and put the dog in a room where he could observe it. What the doctor discovered was more important than how the bandage came off. As soon as the dog removed it he lay down in a patch of sunlight, exposing the wound to its healing rays. The dog was soon cured. From this observation was born Dr. Rollier's idea of using sunlight to heal people.

Many of the little patients whom we saw came from the British Isles where sunlight is limited. We looked at early photographs of their misshapen bones and within a few years' treatment by sunlight they were dancing for us, eager as any youngsters. They wore white floppy hats and white shorts. Dr. Rollier explained that he only used the sunlight before 9 A.M. when there was a preponderance of ultraviolet rays. He insisted that patients keep their heads and back of their necks covered at all times. He deplored the notion of people baking for hours in the sun, and said they were only courting future trouble. "Sunlight," said he, "should be used like most medicines in small doses." By degrees, over a period of days, his patients were finally exposed to the sun for a half hour each on front and back.

The tubercular adults lay face down on specially constructed outdoor beds so that they were able to use their hands to assemble, of all things, gas masks. Thus while healing themselves they were providing the means for others to help themselves in the war that everyone felt was sure to come.

E.F. asked Dr. Rollier if patients were on a special diet. Dr. Rollier replied, "We serve them any food that the sun shines on!"

Eight or nine days later we crossed the channel to England, and from the moment we landed, E.F. was full of enthusiasm to show everything he could. Perhaps seeing his native land through the eyes of two "foreigners" gave him new impetus and pleasure. His energy never sagged. He gave us a running history as we toured through Canterbury, Oxford, and Stratford-on-Avon, so that our heads buzzed with information and our feet ached with overexertion. I think we saw every cathedral and abbey in England.

We drove up along the Cornish coast, dipping into Wales, and the town of Bath where the Romans had established themselves; and so on through towns with unpronounceable Welsh names that, as E.F. explained, usually were descriptive of the place; and sometimes intriguing as Mouse Hole. We stood on the cliff at Land's End which the Romans called Bellerium, looking westward toward

America. E.F. asked Blanche (he was always getting her reaction to things), "What do you feel here?"

She replied, "It's beautiful but melancholy as if there had been a lot of weeping here."

He agreed and then changed the subject a little, saying that England probably would be an icy desert were it not for the beneficence of the Gulf Stream coming from that far-off shore. Later as we passed through Penzance, E.F. sang a song from the Gilbert and Sullivan operetta.

In London we stayed at the Savoy whose accommodations included a bathtub almost the size of a swimming pool. After dinner E.F. decided to read in his room. Blanche decided on a warm bath. I went for a walk. When I returned, she had a typical British story to tell. As she settled in the long tub with an Agatha Christie mystery, she suddenly found herself sliding under the water. Grasping for any support, she took hold of a silver handle hanging on the wall. She pulled herself up by it and settled back again with her soggy novel, when she heard a male voice at the door inquiring discreetly, "Did you ring, *sir*?" That silver handle was a bellcord to summon the servant. In this case *he* answered.

E.F. showed us as much of London as he could in the time we had left. Among our first stops were the Tower of London, St. Paul's Cathedral and Westminster Abbey, and the Houses of Parliament where E.F.'s father had been a member. He told us that his mother was among the first women allowed to sit in the gallery. (In this regard, it is curious that on July 2, 1962, Blanche and Mrs. Dunn, the wife of the barrister who handled the Emmet Fox estate, were among the first women allowed into the Lawyers' Club in Gray's Inn to have lunch, the queen, of course, having been absolutely first. We always felt that E.F. had arranged it.)

Seeing Buckingham Palace and the changing of the guard was a must. E.F. insisted that I take a movie of Blanche walking past the guard in his sentry box. He said, "A visit to London would not be complete without it." Sometimes I felt that E.F. should have been a motion picture director. So often when I was taking pictures he would arrange the details, whether Blanche was sitting on a fence in the Rockies, or in a café in Paris.

He took us into several lecture halls where he had spoken or held meetings in bygone years. Among them were Wigmore Hall where he gave his Sunday evening lectures, and the famous Albert Hall. One afternoon we went away from the center of London to stop in front of a building where a Higher Thought Center had been. E.F. said that the woman who had conducted meetings there had been a schoolteacher, and she ran the meetings as she had her schoolroom. Halfway through the lecture she would stop, open the windows, ask the group to stand, and say, "Breathe in, smell the pines, breathe in health; now exhale your negative ideas." She did the exercise several times, always emphasizing, "Smell the pines." E.F. said she was a good teacher of New Thought, but he could never smell the pines. The only odor he could discern was the aroma of hops being brewed down the street at a brewery. Standing in the street there we noticed the same odor. The brewery was still there; the Higher Thought Center had moved elsewhere.

While standing there we had our first encounter with chimney sweeps. Two of them came down the street in their high hats, carrying brooms and other paraphernalia, and covered with soot from head to toe. E.F. said, "Herman, get your camera. We must get a picture of Blanche with these two." The sweeps were most obliging—and very thoughtful. One stood on each side of her, placing their hands within an inch of her shoulders. E.F. commented, "It wouldn't be London without chimney sweeps." Later in a souvenir shop E.F. bought us a miniature chimney sweep to take home and "he" still resides with us.

Life in London moved at a quick pace. A sandwich and English cider at the Cheshire Cheese, tea on the roof of Selfridge's with a splendid view of London, and in the evening roast beef at Simpson's on the Strand where a huge roast was brought to the table and carved according to choice—absolutely delicious. At night we went to an outdoor performance of Shakespeare's *A Midsummer Night's Dream*. E.F. was very proud of his London. Sunday morning found us in Petticoat Lane where we saw Cockneys sporting their multibuttoned clothing. Petticoat Lane was a series of stalls where secondhand anything was sold. Most of the dealers were honest but because of the crowds there were other types who frequented the place. E.F. said quietly, "This is a place where you can have your watch lifted at one end of the street, and sold back to you at the other." Then he added, "We're good Truth students; so it won't happen to us."

Before we left London he took us for a ride on the underground and told us of a demonstration he had made when he was an electrical engineer working on the technology of the underground. A particular section had been completed and the engineers were ready to turn on the power. Word was passed along for workmen to remove themselves from the area. Although the return all-clear signal was given for the line, E.F. had a very strong feeling that something was amiss. He treated about it and felt that there still was a man who had not been notified of the power turn-on. He insisted that a thorough check be made, which would take a couple of hours. Other crew members called it nonsense and a waste of time. But in fact there was a man who had been working in a sequestered area, and he would have been electrocuted!

The next day Blanche and I left for Liverpool where we were to embark on the *S.S. Samaria,* and three weeks later E.F. returned on the *Queen Mary.*

THE CHANGING FORTIES

Nineteen hundred forty turned out to be another banner year. The Church moved its offices to the Hotel Astor in March; and our meetings recessed for the summer on June 9. Italy declared war on France June 10, and we started on a whirlwind investigative and lecture tour with E.F. on June 18.

On this trip our first stop was at Dr. Kellogg's famous Battle Creek Sanatorium where we met one of his assistants, a Dr. Olson, who conducted Emmet Fox and me through the buildings. E.F. was especially interested in the healing techniques being used, and Dr. Olson explained them, using medical terminology which E.F. easily understood, having grown up with a physician father.

The next day found us at Zion, Illinois, chatting with Mr. and Mrs. Voliva of the Christian Catholic Church. They did not believe in drugs, doctors, smoking, coffee, or alcohol, but they did believe in healing by prayer.

In Davenport, Iowa, we were welcomed by B.J. Palmer, founder of the Chiropractic School of Healing. He knew of E.F. and his healing work, and to this day many chiropractors still recommend the Emmet Fox booklets, such as "The Golden Key" and "The Seven Day Mental Diet," to their patients. B.J., eager to explain his theory of healing, showed us charts and a skeleton of the human body, pointing out the stresses and strains that take place especially in the spinal column. He gave E.F. a chiropractic treatment

to demonstrate the techniques used, in particular sub-
luxating the spine, and freeing the neck and shoulders.

The next day we were at Kirkville, Missouri, the foun-
tainhead of the Osteopathic School of Healing. We spent
the morning going through the hospital and studying its
techniques, similar in respects to chiropractic ones, and
E.F. experienced an osteopathic treatment there. I asked
him how he felt after these treatments, and he said, "Fine!
Very limber," to which I responded, "I think we're going
to have a hard time keeping up with you on this trip!"

Emmet Fox felt that true healing naturally came from
God but that man had found different ways to bring about
that excellent condition, so he left no stone unturned in
his search to understand as much as possible. Above all he
wanted to gain his awareness through actual experience.
As a result, in his lectures he was always speaking from
strength born of firsthand knowledge.

In a couple of days we were at Unity headquarters at
917 Tracy in Kansas City, where we had been so many
times before. E.F. gave a lecture to the workers and the
students, which was followed by lunch with Charles, Cora,
Lowell, and Rick Fillmore. In the afternoon we went to
Unity Farm where a convention was in progress. Margaret
Truman was there and took a few minutes to relax in the
pool. A large number from our own congregation in New
York were also at the farm. E.F. had casually announced at
the last service that he would be speaking at Unity.

Our next stop was Denver where the Divine Science
Summer School was in progress, and E.F. was kept busy
giving lectures to the students and taking the church service on Sunday. Our Denver friends were eager to show us
around. The Denver area is filled with history of the west—
and so was our car. E.F. had amassed a veritable library
about the early days of the west. We visited Buffalo Bill's

grave, and left our blessing on that hero. And we also left our blessing at the Tabor Gold Mine where Baby Doe (Mrs. Tabor) died in a hut.

Then in our healing investigations we went on to the hot baths at Thermopolis, Wyoming, where visitors have gone for relief from rheumatism and other ailments. The baths are at an elevation of over 4,000 feet, and it was interesting that not far away oil was being pumped out of the ground.

Our Denver friends told us that the sunrise from the top of Mt. Washburn in Yellowstone National Park was an unforgettable sight. So E.F. had us on our way at 3:30 A.M. in the dim light and chilly air twisting up a trail barely wide enough for the car. It started to rain and in spite of all our spiritual treatment we never did see the sunrise, but as the Bible says, "God provided some better thing." We saw the most spectacular storm. We were so high up that lightning could be seen between the lower mountain peaks and in the valleys below. We arrived at the hotel in time for a much-needed breakfast, and then the sun came out in all its splendor. All in all quite a show!

South of Yellowstone lie some of the most rugged mountains in the world, the Grand Tetons. While staying there at Jenny Lake Ranch, E.F. thought it would be fun to go horseback riding. He fared better than Blanche and I as he had ridden in Central Park in New York. We set off on the trail toward Lake Solitude, with my horse in the lead. Everything went pretty well for a time except that my horse liked to jog ahead and I found myself holding the reins with one hand and my glasses with the other. Just as we reached a bend in the trail, my horse suddenly whirled around and galloped in the other direction. I got him to face about but he reared up on his hind legs. E.F. rushed up, took hold of the reins, and led him back. As we got around the bend again, we spotted the cause of the panic: a huge bear slouching off through the underbrush.

At Salt Lake City, after visiting the Mormon Tabernacle, we went for a swim in Great Salt Lake. E.F. and I plunged in and found it almost impossible to sink. But the water was very salty, and we were glad to get a fresh shower. Continuing west, we stayed in Reno overnight and were intrigued not only by the bright lights of the gambling casinos, but by the many shop signs as well, which advertised quick marriages and quick divorces (after a proper stay in Reno), and lawyers who were willing to handle both—for a proper fee, naturally.

In a few days after passing through Yosemite Park with its magnificent redwoods, we reached San Francisco and the International New Thought Congress in progress at the Palace Hotel. Most of the metaphysical teachers and ministers were there, including Angela Morgan, poet laureate of the New Thought Movement. And a number of people from New York, of course!

The great ballroom was packed every day, fine talks were delivered, and much healing took place. E.F. was in his natural element. While we were in San Francisco, their World's Fair was going on. It was not so large as New York's but the lighting effects were extremely beautiful and startling. E.F. was invited to speak at the Fair in the Temple of Religion. We did a lot of sightseeing and attended all the lectures as well.

One evening a newspaperwoman invited us to dinner at a Japanese restaurant. According to custom, we had to remove our shoes at the door and E.F. began to feel uncomfortable. We sat on the floor around the brazier and a "geisha" girl served the food, which we ate with chopsticks. Although it was unique, it added to E.F.'s discomfort and in a few moments he asked for a chair. The waiter brought a stool. And it was not long before he asked for a knife and fork. The food was delicious when one could manage to snag it somehow with the chopsticks. Later E.F. said, "If we ever get to Japan we'll only go to restaurants where they have standard equipment!" (No one knew then that in a year's time Japan would be at war with us.)

Leaving San Francisco, we stopped in at the Rosicrucians where we found others from New York were doing the same thing. We stayed at Asilomar near Monterey and Pacific Grove. The beauty of the Pacific coast is indescribable. The next day we were in Los Angeles and E.F. was constantly recognized wherever we went. He had so many commitments in Los Angeles and there was so much to see and do that sometimes we did not get back to the hotel until after midnight.

In addition to all the usual tourist attractions, we visited Angelus Temple presided over by Aimee Semple McPherson, the dynamic leader and healer who was at her zenith. E.F. had said, "Before we meet Aimee in person, let's attend her healing meeting." Blanche was wearing a large "halo" hat and when Aimee came out, her first request was, "Will that young lady with the big hat please take it off so that the others in back can see me." We regretted that we did not think of it ourselves.

In her long white robes and auburn hair, Aimee was a statuesque beauty. She began the service. There was a lot of hymn singing "to prepare the atmosphere" and then individuals were brought on the platform to be healed of illnesses as Aimee prayed and the congregation sang. It was an unusual experience. The service lasted three hours, and toward the end a collection was taken. Aimee put her hands to her ears and said, "A silent collection, please!" E.F. whispered, "That's the best kind!"

The next day we met Aimee. She was excited about

meeting E.F. and knew of him and his books. She was very gracious and showed us around the Temple.

Before leaving Los Angeles we went to the large Seventh Day Adventist camp to hear a lecture under a huge tent, and once again to fill up the back of the car with more books. The next day we headed east through the Mojave Desert with its own unusual beauty, and spent the night in Las Vegas. There were the gambling casinos (not as plush as today), cowboys, Indians, and prostitutes in scanty attire in the doorways on side streets. E.F. commented, "This is the west I read about in England. This could only happen in America."

In a couple of days we were on the North Rim of the Grand Canyon, at Bright Angel Point, one of the most majestically beautiful spots in the world. As far as the eye could see were escarpments carved by the Colorado River, a ribbon of silver in the distance. The colors were fantastic —mauve, magenta, blue, gold, burnt orange—and all changed in hue as the sun moved its position. E.F. delighted in suggesting angles for the pictures I was taking, but I have never yet seen any reproduction that could do justice to the Grand Canyon. Its immensity and grandeur stagger the mind and have to be seen to be believed.

At the Lodge we had a couple of surprises awaiting us. As we entered the lobby, Dale Carnegie greeted us warmly and remarked, "Surely this place lifts the spirit!" To which E.F. laughingly replied, "This is a good place to stop worrying and start living!" When Dale Carnegie autographed his book to Emmet Fox, he wrote: "Few—if any—have done more than you have to help people stop worrying and start living. I have enjoyed your books immensely. May God keep on loving you always."

The waitresses at the Lodge were Mormon college girls from Salt Lake City. At dinner, the young lady serving us asked, "Aren't you Emmet Fox?"

"Yes, how did you know?"

"Oh," she said, "you're *The Sermon on the Mount* man. I recognized you from the picture on your book!"

After a few days of communing with God in that beautifully tranquil setting, E.F. suggested we drive to the South Rim of the Canyon for a different aspect. The Canyon is eighteen miles wide at that point, but to reach the South Rim requires a drive of 200 miles. There was only one point where we could cross the mighty Colorado and that was near Lees Ferry at Navajo Bridge situated high up on the plateau. We started out on a clear crisp day. The nearest habitation was a gas station forty-four miles away with the rather Biblical name of Jacob Lake.

We had gone thirty miles when the car simply went dead on the road. Nothing I did could get it started. E.F. said, "Well, this is a time for treatment." We sat, prayed for a few moments, blessing the car and its occupants, and then E.F. said, "Try the motor again." It started up in a flash. With the practicality of the true metaphysician, he added, "Let's stop at Jacob Lake and see if the mechanic there can find out what the trouble was." We did just that, and after waiting for an hour while he took the carburetor apart, we were told, "That kind of thing often happens on the dusty roads."

From there we took what was perhaps the worst wagon trail in the United States, but the scenery was magnificent with boulders as big as a house. We passed by some small Indian camps and cliffs of brilliant vermillion. At one place we had to go through a small stream—no bridge—and I felt the car shudder once or twice. We took pictures when we finally reached Navajo Bridge, and then headed south about seventy miles' distant to an Indian trading post at Cameron.

Every once in awhile the motor skipped a beat, but my passengers did not notice, so entranced were they with the exquisite colors of the Painted Desert. Sunset came and Cameron was still thirty miles away when the motor again went dead. We treated but the motor would not start. I got out and opened the hood, hoping I could do something. Instead it started to rain. It was as if error were throwing everything it had at us.

Undaunted, E.F. said, "Man's extremity is God's opportunity. Let's put our weight on God." We silently prayed together for perhaps ten minutes. E.F. said, "Let's try it again," and once more the motor started up; and as if by divine direction I put my fingers on a wire under the dash. It was hot because it was loose. A simple turn of the nut holding it remedied the difficulty and we had no more trouble with the car. It was now dark and I kept it going at high speed until we saw one lone electric light in the distance. We called it "the star of the East"—the star of revelation—even though we were heading south, and we gave thanks for the revelation we had had.

The place was Cameron and that evening we put our names in the same register where princes and presidents had placed theirs. It was really an Indian trading post with accommodations for guests in this wonderful wilderness. Dark-skinned Navajo Indians wearing brilliant turquoise jewelry were everywhere. E.F. remarked, "I wouldn't have missed this for anything."

At breakfast the next morning we looked out the window and saw a long line of Navajos on ponies wearily riding along a ridge. E.F. asked the proprietor where they were going. He said they were heading back to their hogans after having spent the last few days with their medicine man trying to heal one of their tribesmen. Unfortunately, the man had died. E.F. said to us, "Let's bless our Indian brother. He'll know more in his new incarnation."

At the trading post we saw beautiful turquoise jewelry

on sale that had been pawned by Navajos for cash to pay their bills. E.F. asked Blanche to pick something out. She thought it was meant as a gift for someone else, and chose an attractive silver bracelet with large turquoise stones in it. Then he said, "I want you to keep it as a souvenir of this remarkable outpost of civilization." Through the years Blanche and I learned that Emmet Fox was a deeply sensitive and sentimental man.

We heard the unmistakable sound of "one-armed bandits" at the Post, being played by Navajos who were pumping in coin after coin and not winning. After awhile our little imp, Blanche, drew a nickel out of her purse, slipped it into one of the machines, and a flood of nickels spilled onto the floor. The Navajos looked with amazement, then helped her pick them up. Blanche counted seven Indians helping, turned to E.F., and asked, "Isn't seven divine fulfillment?" E.F. laughed and said, "No metaphysical skullduggery, please!" She divided the nickels among the seven Indians, and E.F. said, "No more gambling for you."

We proceeded toward the South Rim, and the next morning when E.F. found we could go down to the bottom on muleback, off we went along a narrow trail that hugged the precipitous walls. Mules are very surefooted and not easily scared, but they did walk along the edge of the trail, kicking stones over that rattled down into the depths. The guide had told us that so long as we held on to the mule we had nothing to worry about. But pretty soon E.F. asked, "Why do these mules insist on walking on the outside. I would feel more comfortable if they walked on the inside."

The cowboy replied, "That's where you are not as smart as the mule. There are two good reasons why he is on the outside. He knows you are on his back and that on the inside you might be thrown off by protruding rocks along the wall. But even more important, the rattlers around here like to sun themselves on little ledges and anything that passed near them they would strike at."

As we reached the halfway point of Indian Gardens, we stopped to eat our boxed lunch. The guide shot a rattler that was under the watering trough for the mules. We learned that nature has given rattlesnakes of the Grand Canyon a slightly pinkish cast to blend with the coloration of the rocks and protect them from eagles and hawks whose prey they are.

It was late afternoon when we reached Phantom Ranch, a tropical paradise beside the Colorado River. We were so saddlesore from the trail ride that we had to be helped off the mules. We were glad to have the hotel management lend us bathing suits, and the three of us jumped into the pool. It felt good. When we had time to look around we saw the immense grandeur surrounding us. The Colorado River, which had seemed a little silver ribbon from the rim, was now a roaring torrent, and we looked up at the fantastic shapes thousands of feet above us. Going up to the rim the next day was harder on the mules than on us.

Before leaving the South Rim E.F. suggested a plane ride over the Canyon "to see where we had been." It was one of the most thrilling experiences we had ever had. From the tiny airstrip, miles from the edge of the Canyon, we flew about a thousand feet above a plateau, and then suddenly we were over the Canyon with 6,000 feet between us and terra firma. The views were magnificent as we circled over this wonderland of nature, but as we headed back toward the airstrip, we were confronted by huge black clouds and torrential rain that obscured our vision. E.F. came to our rescue: "Let's know that God is opening our way. There is no obstruction in God. God is the pilot of this plane, and underneath are the Everlasting

Arms." The pilot made another wide circle over the Canyon, and just as suddenly as they gathered the clouds parted and we made a quick "dive" toward the landing strip about twenty miles away. We thanked God for His loving protection. It was a very small plane and a very big canyon.

In 1941 great changes came to America and to the rest of the world as well. For Emmet Fox and his work the change came with a startling impact on Sunday, December 7. At our usual Sunday morning service at the Manhattan Opera House in New York, Emmet Fox spoke on the prophetic subject "Light in Darkness." His planned topic for the next Sunday was "The Strange New Things Coming to America."

On this same Sunday, December 7, E.F. was to speak at two different times in Washington, D.C., at the Metropolitan Presbyterian Church at 5 P.M. on "Christ and Anti-Christ," and at 8 P.M. on "The Search for God." We left New York about 1 P.M. and headed down through New Jersey.

It was not long before police cars with screeching sirens were racing in every direction. We turned on the radio and were shocked to learn, between claims and counter-claims, that the Japanese had bombed Pearl Harbor in a surprise attack. E.F. said, "Let's stop at the first place we come to, have a spot of tea, and see if we can find out anything." Police and state troopers were everywhere, and several times our car was checked at roadblocks. At the diner where we stopped, the police rushed in, found an Oriental dishwasher, and hauled him out without further ado. Others were being rounded up from the farms. It seemed like chaos was all around us.

When we returned to the car, E.F. said, "I've been treating about this and I am sure you have too. But let's just stay here a few minutes while we pray together." When he spoke again he seemed disturbed and serious. "Things look very bad for both Europe and America. There are very dark days ahead. It will last longer than most people think. It will need a lot of prayer on both sides of the curtain."

We thought he was referring to the countries on opposite sides in the war. He said, "No. There are of course good people in Germany and Italy and Japan who are praying just as earnestly as we. I was referring to those that have passed on. Their prayers can be very helpful, and we should not hesitate to ask their prayerful help when we think of them." He continued, "America will win. There is no question about that, but when the war is over it will not be the world we know. Eventually it will be a better world for millions of people."

As we went on, the sirens and the excitement continued, and we were wondering what bedlam would await us in Washington. When we got there, however, there was utter calm and peace. It was as if the whole town were having an afternoon siesta.

As one might expect, more people came to the lectures than the church auditorium could hold.

On the following Sunday, December 14, E.F. arrived at the Manhattan Opera House in New York to find the hall packed with people. Police were outside directing the flow of the large crowds trying to get in. E.F. began his talk with a text from Chapter 40 of the book of Isaiah: "Comfort ye, comfort ye my people, saith your God. . . . They that wait upon the Lord shall renew their strength; they shall mount up with wings as eagles; they shall run, and not be weary; and they shall walk, and not faint." He continued: "It is indeed remarkable that on our Guest Sunday, the first for quite a long time, we have probably the largest crowd* in our experience, including the ball-room upstairs, and undoubtedly the largest crowd which has ever come together in the metaphysical movement.

"This has been a week of destiny, the most momentous week in American history since the signing of the Declaration of Independence. The American people today are united as they have never been before in their history, even in the great days of Revolutionary fervor. Never, even in Washington's time, were people so completely united, unselfishly resolved, as they are today."

As his words echoed across the great hall and by microphone hooked into the upstairs ballroom, the entire audience rose and applauded. We learned that in times of stress, such as those days were, people who were not ordinarily churchgoers flocked to the meetings.

As the war continued, shortages of gasoline and tires developed, and rationing began. The gasoline shortage affected us most. Although E.F. could have used his influence to get an adequate supply, he refused to do so even though he had many speaking commitments around the country. He felt everyone should do his share. So we traveled a great deal by plane. Sometimes we were "bumped" off flights by military priorities, as happened on our 1944 trip to the International New Thought Convention in Louisville, Kentucky. We were bumped in Cleveland and had to make hurried rearrangements and make the rest of the trip by train. E.F. never minded these minor inconveniences, quietly "treating" each situation as it occurred.

One effect the war produced was an increase in the number of marriages Emmet Fox performed. There were also great shifts of population into the military and into defense plants around the country. This meant many new

* Over 8,000 people.

faces in our audience. The stress the nation was under seemed to inspire Emmet Fox to even greater heights, and he brought comfort and solace to thousands.

With the war over, in 1946 E.F. wanted to fly to England but civilian travel was still being discouraged, so we took the second trip to Mexico instead, during which E.F. further researched Mexican symbolism. From then on we resumed our yearly treks. Emmet Fox continued his search for basic Truth. As he often said, he would pay any price and go anywhere to get a lift in consciousness, and he spent a good part of his life and his wealth in doing just that. It was a joy for Blanche and me to be part of it.

The
Psychic-Spiritual
Side

I want to open this chapter on the Psychic-Spiritual Side by giving a quotation from Emmet Fox himself. He cautions: "Do not dabble in psychic things. If you wish to investigate thoroughly and scientifically, well and good, but this will be the work of years, and will call for scientific conditions. The chief objection to the running after mediums that so many people practice is that it is really a running away from the responsibilities of this life."

Emmet Fox began his psychic research in London at the British Society for Psychical Research where he took part in a number of psychic experiments. It was his opinion that verifiable results could only be obtained where the same persons sat together for a number of sessions. I believe this condition was also mentioned during the experiments held at Duke University. As a result of his research E.F. in time appeared on the same platform with Sir Oliver Lodge and Sir Arthur Conan Doyle at Albert Hall in London before a huge audience. Emmet Fox emerged as "the star of the evening," and the newspaper publicity about it led to a family confrontation which his sister Nora recounted to us.

According to Nora, "a neighborly busybody" could not wait to gossip about the news with Mrs. Fox, E.F.'s mother. Said this talebearer, "Is this your Emmet that's in all the papers speaking on a new religion?" (Both she and the Fox family were Roman Catholics.) And then she went on at length about the details. Mrs. Fox, a woman of stature and dignity, composed herself and walked away without saying a word.

Later that day when E.F. came home, Mrs. Fox asked, "Emmet, is it true what they are saying about you speaking on another religion?"

Emmet replied, "Yes, mother, it is."

His mother asked, "How could you?"

His simple answer was, "Would you have me go against my convictions?"

"All right," she replied, "we'll never speak of the subject again." And they never did.

E.F. continued his psychic research in America and sat with several well-known mediums. Arthur Ford mentions Emmet Fox in his book, *Nothing So Strange*.* He writes:

"Emmet Fox was a minister who took the New Testament record at its face value. It was while I was on my second visit to London, living in Horace Leaf's house, that he first came to see me. Before that time I had never heard of him and he told me nothing about his metaphysical interests until after the sitting. But through Fletcher** some of his own people, discarnates, came to him that day and urged him to accept an invitation he had just received to take over a group in New York City. Fox was much amazed that his unseen friends knew of his offer and de-

---

* New York: Harper & Row, 1958, p. 231.
** Fletcher was a discarnate personality who functioned as Arthur Ford's permanent partner on the unseen plane.

cided to accept the invitation. During the years when he was speaking to his enormous audiences in New York we met often; as a matter of fact we lived in the same hotel for two years and had many discussions both of his work and my own. He expected anyone who accepted the metaphysical system which he taught—which he always felt was simply the metaphysics of Jesus—to take for granted the survival of personality and the flow of communication between the living and the dead."

He also worked with two or three highly respected astrologers who drew his charts in detail, and he was impressed by the resemblance each had to the other. As his popularity grew and his interest in astrology became known, many amateur astrologers came to the meetings and often asked, "What is your birth date?" He handled these inquiries lightly at first. But as the question became more frequent, his humor took over, and he answered with whatever date came to mind. As a result he had astrological readings for a birthday every month of the year.

I believe that these psychic and astrological investigations confirmed a feeling he had had in England long before he came to America: that 1939 would be a crucial year for him. Now, whether an idea is karmic in origin or is the result of "suggestion," whatever we hold deeply in consciousness, we demonstrate. Nineteen hundred and thirty-nine did turn out to be a crucial year for him. Some may say, "Why didn't he eliminate this with treatment." In other words, "Physician, heal thyself!" As Charles Fillmore has often said, "Everyone can see further than he can jump." Be that as it may, the feeling that 1939 would be the year undoubtedly was a prime factor in his urge to get the message to the largest number of people he could in the time allotted. "God sometimes works in mysterious ways his wonders to perform."

Angela Morgan, with her great interest in New Thought, captures what I am trying to say in her beautiful poem, "When Nature Wants a Man": *

> When Nature wants to drill a man
> And thrill a man,
> And skill a man,
> When Nature wants to mould a man
> To play the noblest part;
> When she yearns with all her heart
> To create so great and bold a man
> That all the world shall praise—
> Watch her methods, watch her ways!

Before we go on to 1939, let us get back to the psychic-spiritual side. It really began when the three of us, Emmet Fox, Blanche, and I, gathered in his office to pray and treat together for special cases. At first we took turns treating aloud, but after a time we found we got better and quicker results by doing silent work.

It was during this period E.F. discovered that Blanche had latent psychic ability. He did not mention it at the time, but the first "experiment" occurred one evening when Blanche and I were at the movies. Suddenly in the middle of the movie Blanche whispered to me, "I think E.F. wants you to call him." I was surprised: "At this time of night?" "Well," she said, "I have a strong feeling that he needs spiritual help." So we sat silently and treated him for a few moments. By the time we got home it was near midnight, and I did not call him until the next morning, when I explained what had happened. He asked the particulars

*From *Forward, March!* by Angela Morgan. Reprinted by permission of Dodd, Mead & Co.

of actual time and other circumstances—he always kept precise records—and then said the treatment we made was a good one. He had a pain in his head which soon cleared. It was then he said, "From now on when Blanche or you get these feelings we shall call them 'signals,'" and he asked Blanche to keep a definite record of time, date, conditions, and all details.

That was the beginning of many "experiments" in telepathy, psychometry, absent healing, and other forms of psychic and spiritual healing. As E.F. and Blanche developed their psychic rapport she was able to pinpoint a difficulty, a need, or a mental request. It was not a one-way street by any means, for there were many occasions when E.F. did the same for us, even though we were separated by considerable distances.

One time this happend during a winter recess of the Church. The three of us often went to Florida. E.F. loved the warm sunny climate there but did not particularly like the long car ride since he felt he could use the time to better advantage in New York. Consequently Blanche and I would start earlier in the car, and he would fly to Jacksonville or Miami; we followed the same procedure on the return trip. On one of these journeys, as we headed north, Blanche and I ran into a sleeting snowstorm. As night approached we decided to stop at the first hotel or motel we found. (In those days motels were few and far between.) But the snow was so heavy and the ice on the windshield so thick that visibility was shortened to the point of zero. We only had time to say, "God! God!" when a black void opened in front of us. I jammed on the brakes; the car skidded but held. In the blinding snowstorm we had not seen the Y-fork in the road. We should have turned left or right. We gave fervent thanks for our deliverance, and inched our way back on the right road. Soon we reached a town offering a warm, friendly hotel. Nothing ever looked so good to us.

A couple of weeks later I was working with E.F. at the office when he suddenly pulled out a small notebook and asked, "Were you and Blanche in trouble at 7:45 P.M. a week ago Wednesday?" I thought a moment and remembered the near-accident on the road, and I told him the story. He replied, "Let's call up Blanche and see what her diary says." The time on her record was 7:45 P.M. He told me then, "At that time a flash came to me that you two were in great danger and I immediately claimed divine protection for you." And I again thanked God.

This psychic-spiritual relationship continued through all our years of association. Whenever he needed help or wanted to get in touch with us, if we were not near a telephone where we could be called, he would send a "signal" and Blanche would pick it up.

For most of the time in New York E.F. lived at the Park Central Hotel (now the Park Sheraton). He had thousands of books in a room in his apartment set aside as his library. The titles were catalogued by a friend who at the time was the chief librarian for J.P. Morgan's private (now public) library on East 36th Street and Madison Avenue.

One day E.F. asked us to have lunch with him at the Park Central, during which he said he had something to show us. It was his new, large penthouse apartment with a magnificent view of the New York skyline and the Hudson River. The apartment was empty except for a few shelves near the door with about a dozen books on them. Before going in he asked me to wait outside the door for a moment and he went ahead with Blanche.

He said, "I would like to know what feeling you have about this apartment." I could hear her say, "Oh, it's a beautiful apartment, but I felt a shudder as I came through the door." He asked her to return outside with her back to the door. He was gone for a moment, and then called her in again. "How do you feel now?" he asked. She replied, "Everything feels fine now. I get a very good feeling about the apartment." He went into another room and returned with a book. Blanche gave a little shudder again. He then explained that the book was about ritual murders performed by the aborigines of Iona Island off the coast of Scotland. He had planned the experiment to see what Blanche's reaction would be. It was a form of psychometry, that is, the psychic measure of a person, place, or thing.

On one of our trips we visited the Spiritualist Camp at Lily Dale in New York. The grounds were spacious with lovely old trees, a hotel, a large central meeting hall, a number of bungalows, and apart from the rest, the original cottage of the two Fox sisters (no relationship to Emmet Fox) who founded American spiritualism. This cottage had been moved from its locale in another part of the state to Lily Dale. As we entered the gate to Lily Dale and purchased the necessary admittance tickets, I asked for four, although there were only three of us in the car. At the moment it seemed just a slip of the tongue, but we were soon to find out otherwise.

Our first stop was the Fox sisters' cottage where the woman in charge had the same phase of mediumship as the Fox sisters, namely the ability to answer questions through the intervention of a spirit "guide" with rappings or knocks. As we entered the room, she said, "I see another person with you, a man, one who has recently passed on!" She gave a short description and said, "His name is George." E.F. gave a start but said nothing. She went on to say that we could ask some questions if we liked. These were answered by one knock for yes, and two for no. The raps seemed to come from a stairway that led to the bed-room where the Fox sisters had slept. It was an open ladder-type staircase; so it was impossible for anyone to hide there. Satisfied with the medium's psychic ability, we left.

It was not until the next day when we stopped at the nearest Western Union office to collect forwarded tele-grams that E.F. learned his close friend in London had passed on a few days earlier. There were many of these psychic-spiritual experiences in New York and during our travels in the United States and abroad.

Once on a trip to New England we went from Plymouth Rock to the Christian Science Mother Church in Boston. While there E.F. had a deep desire to visit the birthplace of Mary Baker Eddy and we drove to Bow, New Hamp-shire. As we entered Mrs. Eddy's house, Blanche and I were delighted to be in the presence of two great spiritual leaders, one on either side of the invisible curtain. In the upstairs bedroom was a rocker, a type of chair for which Blanche has a fondness, and which E.F. showed great in-terest in. We stood there a moment in silence, blessing this humble abode, when E.F. said, "Blanche, I would like you to sit in that rocker." She did. "What do you feel?" he asked. And she replied, "I have a very good feeling. A lot of prayers were said here, and a lot of questions asked."

On our trip to Europe in 1937 our first overnight stop was in Caen, France, at the Hotel Angleterre. After dinner we took a walk through the dimly lighted town. Suddenly Blanche stopped and E.F. asked, "What do you see, Blanche?" She replied, "I see soldiers fighting in the streets with bayonets. They are right in front of us." Even though I was used to this sort of conversation between E.F. and Blanche, the words were so dramatic that I looked up star-tled but saw nothing. E.F. replied, "I see it too. There will be a terrible battle here and it needs a lot of prayer." We stopped for a few moments and claimed God's blessing for that place.

We returned to the hotel and went to bed. During the night, Blanche awakened me. "There is shooting going on in the hotel, and soldiers going through the rooms," she said. I tried to soothe her, but I felt a little uneasy myself. "But," she continued, "I know it's going to happen." In the morning at breakfast we found that E.F. had spent most of the night in prayer and treatment, for he had had the same feelings and said that the battle would be more terrible than he had at first thought.

(What Blanche and E.F. had felt that night actually did happen seven years later on D-Day during the Allies' invasion of France. There was much death and destruction in and around that area in the battles that followed.)

The next day we left for Paris and the start of our trip around Europe. When we met in the lobby that morning, E.F. said he had a feeling of impending danger concerning himself. Blanche and I felt similar "signals." There was nothing to do but pray and take what care we could. It was not a dreadful feeling, as such, but rather that something was going to happen. Day after day we treated about this, using the 91st Psalm in particular as E.F. always recommended it for protection. (During the war he constantly suggested it to the parents and wives of men in the service as a daily prayer and meditation. There were many wonderful reports of "miraculous" results.)

In addition I was especially careful while driving, and we took extra precautions in all our moving about. Still, the negative feeling never entirely left us, although the weight of it seemed to lighten. We had a grand tour all the way to Rome and on our way back to Zurich in Switzerland to visit Dr. Jung. We left his villa in the afternoon, and E.F. wanted to stay that night at Montreux on Lake Geneva, a favorite spot for the three of us. But it got to be 9 P.M., and we decided to stop at the town of Martignyville instead. It was there that the premonition of danger we had had, revealed itself.

E.F. was the first to walk toward the Hotel Kluser. Over the entrance was an immense chandelier, and as E.F. was about to enter the hotel, there was the sudden earsplitting crash of this chandelier at his feet. One inch closer and it would have hit him directly. Although we were all shaken by what happened, all further "signals" disappeared. E.F. felt that our combined prayers had saved his life and that if we could have risen just a little higher in consciousness, the thing would not have happened at all. We enjoyed the rest of the trip without incident.

Eventually the year 1939 arrived. As E.F. had prophesied, this would be the year of crisis in his life. All through the years he felt he had very special work to do (not in an egotistical way) and only a limited time in which to do it. This was why he gave so much time to his search for Truth.

In March 1939 the critical period began. Blanche was receiving more and more spiritual "signals" from E.F. He depended a great deal on our spiritual treatments. On April 9, Easter Sunday, E.F. announced to the large congregation that he needed a rest and that the Church would close for the season. An audible sigh of concern rippled through the congregation, and as members passed him at the door, each promised to pray for him.

The next morning E.F. called us to say he wanted to leave town immediately and be relieved of all the pressures of work: the crisis had arrived. I told him of a quiet place in upper New York State, the town of Oneonta that had a good hotel. It was there that the "overcoming" took place. We arrived about four in the afternoon, and after a short rest, went down to the dining room. E.F. ate practically nothing, but he kept talking to us, unfolding, as it were, a karmic record of his life.* Finally he said, "If I get through this night, I will have a number of years to carry on." We went up to our room to pray and treat. He stayed with us for about an hour, saying nothing. When he left to go to his own room, his only words were, "Keep praying until you get a real sense of the Presence of God."

We started reading the Gideon Bible that was on the dresser. (We have blessed the Gideons many times for their thoughtfulness in providing these Bibles.) We selected certain passages and used them as treatments. Among the texts, we chose the 91st Psalm again: "A thousand shall fall at thy side, and ten thousand at thy right hand; but it shall not come nigh thee." Another was Jesus' statement: "I am come that they might have life, and that they might have it more abundantly" (John 10:10). And the text from the 46th Psalm: "God is our refuge and strength, a very present help in trouble. . . . Be still, and know that I am God." There were others too. We prayed for hours. Finally a sense of peace came as the heaviness lifted and we went to sleep.

Some time later Blanche woke and called out to me, "There's a great white light in the room and Emmet Fox is standing in it." I saw the vision too as it slowly faded. I got up and went to E.F.'s room. As I knocked on his door, he called out, "Yes, I know. The crisis has passed and all is well."

We slept late the next morning, and were a happy group at breakfast. Blanche and I recounted our experience of the night before, and E.F. said that he knew what had

*The reader is urged to reread Emmet Fox's own account of the "unfolding of the Judgment Books" in the chapter, "Reincarnation and Life After Death."

happened. The Bible calls it the "alighting of the dove," a very rare experience in life, which means that the demonstration has been made. He explained that he was to have died when he was a young man but that prayer had saved him. Now he expressed gratitude to Blanche and me for having helped him through this crisis. There was a sad note. He added that there would be a third time and that it would be harder to overcome.

Departure

The year 1951 proved to be the third time in Emmet Fox's life when it would be more difficult to keep him on this plane. The first part of the year was a period of rest for E.F., a sabbatical, and with the approach of June the three of us were looking forward to another sojourn in Europe. We shipped our car ahead on a freighter, and two weeks later were aboard a flight to Europe via Gander and Shannon and then on to London. After a good "Irish" breakfast in Shannon, the captain told us to expect storms on the way to London. Immediately E.F. said to us, "Let's not believe it. God is in charge of this plane." And He was; we had smooth flying all the way. After ten days of sightseeing in London, we flew to Paris and later picked up our car at Dunkerque.

E.F. seemed to enjoy Paris more than ever. He was anxious to have another look at the famed cathedral at Chartres with its beautiful stained-glass windows; then down to Orléans made famous by Joan of Arc. Returning to Paris, we went once again to view the golden statue of Joan mounted on her horse. Another day we went out to Reims, passing the battlefields of World War I. We often stopped at those places where men on either side of the conflict had fought and died. We also blessed the Père Lachaise Cemetery in Paris, and it seemed strange to Blanche and me that E.F. wanted to go there several times.

On the lighter side, one of E.F.'s friends invited us to see a "collection" of the latest fashions with chic models in stunning gowns. That evening E.F. said to us with a twinkle in his eye, "There are collections and collections, depending whether you are sitting in Dior's or in church!"

On several occasions we drove slowly through the narrow streets of La Cité, the small island in the Seine where many French celebrities had lived. Some of the buildings have plaques on them, listing the names of past tenants. After four or five days of this E.F. explained that there were "two unfinished pieces of business" that he wanted to write of. One was an article on La Cité; the other was a brochure on George Washington as he saw him.

"In the accounts of Washington I read as a child," E.F. said, "he was not like anything on earth. Children were told ridiculous stories about him. He was presented to the world foolishly, as a man who was cold, perfect, unsympathetic, no human weaknesses whatever. Then about thirty or forty years ago, the tide turned. There was a reaction. The debunkers came along and when they were through it turned out that he was not a great man at all.

"But now there is a third phase to Washington's life. I believe that Washington was one of the greatest generals of all time. I believe that he was one of the greatest men who ever lived. Washington never used the language of religion or spiritual things; he was a soldier. But he had it, and much more than many people who were using the language."

On Saturday, August 11, Paris was in a gay mood. People were beginning the festivities that would culminate on

August 15 in the celebration by Roman Catholics of the Feast of the Assumption of the Virgin Mary. As for the three of us, E.F. thought it a good idea to change our routine slightly and have lunch in the elegance of the Grand Hotel. When E.F. asked the young waiter who seemed to be new at the job what kind of fish was available, he answered, "Water fish." E.F. laughed heartily and remarked to us, "What other kind is there?" I replied facetiously, "Flying fish!"

After lunch we retired to the quiet of the Grand Salon. E.F. said, "Let's have a silent meditation together." After awhile he commented, "I feel that was a very good meditation," and then he began to review his life. Once or twice we tried to interrupt, but he went right on. At one point he saddened us by saying, "I have given all I have to the people. Now it is up to them to carry on." As he continued speaking it sounded more and more as if he were going to stop working, although only a couple of weeks before he had sent a telegram to the board of trustees, saying he would be back in the pulpit in the fall.

He continued, "We three have lived many times before and it is not by accident that we are together in this life. I have often thought of past lives and at times ancient Egypt comes into focus, and at other times Greece and especially the Acropolis seems very vivid"—although he had never been to either place. Blanche then added she always felt she had lost her life once in a previous incarnation by drowning. "I remember being in a small boat but different than the ones we see now. It was on a river and a moonlit night and mountains around. When I try to remember more a curtain comes down, but I always feel it was Egypt and I would like to go there." E.F. responded, "You and Herman will make it, but I won't."

(His prediction would come true seventeen years later,

when I was asked to conduct a Holy Land Tour with side trips to Cairo, the Pyramids, and Luxor. When we arrived at Cairo and the beautiful flowing Nile, I waited for Blanche to react to whatever might seem familiar to her. She did do something very odd for her. As we left the bus to pick up the camels that were to take us to the Sphinx and Pyramids, Blanche ran to a particular camel and said, "This one is mine!" as if she had known it all her life. She could not explain her action afterward except to say, "I've been here many times before." In a couple of days we took a plane to Luxor to see Tutankhamen's tomb. As we walked along the Nile in the early evening with the moon shining brightly in the cloudless sky, Blanche suddenly exclaimed, "This is the place I told E.F. about so long ago.")

At that moment in Paris, sitting with E.F. in the Salon at the Grand Hotel, our thoughts were only about his well being. He brightened up as he came out of his reverie, and we returned to the Chateau Frontenac. At seven o'clock we went to dinner at La Coupole in Montparnasse. After dinner we drove up the Champs Élysées slowly at his request. At that time of year Paris is light until 9:30 P.M. He was in good spirits and the town was in a holiday mood. He asked Blanche to sing "Roses of Picardy," and soon he was singing along. It was a perfect evening. We circled around the Étoile as the electric lights sparkled like diamonds in a necklace. Then E.F. humorously observed that it was getting past his bedtime. He suggested we drop him off at the hotel and we stay out longer and enjoy ourselves. The plan was to meet in the hotel lobby at 1 P.M. next day.

At 1 P.M. he did not appear, but we were not concerned as we thought he might have gone for a walk. However, his room key was not with the concierge. We waited a half hour and when there was no response to our telephone call, we decided to ask the concierge to let us into his room. We found E.F. lying in the bed with his Bible resting on his chest and the lights still on. We tried to waken him but could not. (Later, when we had time to think, we found it strange that neither of us had received any "signals" from him, as was the usual procedure whenever he had any difficulty.) It was urgent to find a doctor immediately. Because of the holiday weekend, however, it was almost impossible to locate one, and only after many telephone calls by the concierge did a doctor finally arrive. He told us that E.F.'s pulse, blood pressure, and heart were functioning well but that he was in a coma and should be taken to a hospital immediately. Blanche and I went with him in the ambulance to the American Hospital in Paris where to our relief we found an English-speaking doctor in charge. He was very sympathetic and told us to keep in touch with him.

At two in the afternoon, August 13, Emmet Fox took his departure from this side of the curtain. But not before, the doctor told us, he sat up in bed and started to give a lecture! Blanche and I stood at his bedside and looked at our friend. There was a beautiful smile on his face. He was radiant and looked twenty years younger. We kissed him and said, "We'll be seeing you." (And we still do. We see him with the eyes of the spirit, and his presence is a continuing source of inspiration and a constant help to us and to many others who experience him as we do, metaphysical teachers among them.)

Then the American Embassy took charge. They informed us that an autopsy by the French authorities had to be performed as E.F. had not been under a doctor's care. Everyone was most solicitous and offered whatever help was needed. In due course the authorities found the cause of death to be a cerebral hemorrhage.

Emmet Fox was cremated in his beloved Père Lachaise Cemetery, but not until his sister, Nora Fox, arrived in Paris with a friend to give her permission. In spite of the somber circumstances she found a light moment of humor as her illustrious brother often had. When she realized what great work Emmet Fox had accomplished, for he always underplayed his fame so as not to hurt her Catholic sensitivities, she said to us and an embassy official standing by, "Fancy him starting a new religion when we've got a perfectly good one!" We could not help but laugh.

It was not until we received the ashes and had them on board the *Ile de France*, the ship he loved so much, that we began to receive "signals" from him again. The three of us had a wonderful crossing.

On August 13 Blanche had written in her diary: "Dear Dr. Fox, from the beautiful smile on your face today, I know that you know that all the things you taught are true. How wonderful for you! You always said 13 was your 'lucky' number. Continue to bless us. I shall always sing 'Roses of Picardy' for you as I did the last time we were together." As we boarded the *Ile de France*, the orchestra was playing that tune.

Newspapers in Europe and America, and metaphysical magazines and periodicals, carried the news. I think the most beautiful tribute came from Dr. Fletcher Harding, writing in the *Science of Mind* magazine:

"On Monday, August 13, 1951, the earthly sojourn of Dr. Emmet Fox came to a quiet end, in his beloved Paris, where he began the experience of which he had written to comfort uncounted thousands in his booklet 'Life After Death.'

"Seekers of Truth throughout the entire world will reverently pause to pay tribute to this noble soul whose life was marked with rich achievement. Those who hunger and thirst after righteousness will treasure his books for generations to come. His *Sermon on the Mount* has been carried by praying hands into every church. His *Find and Use Your Inner Power* has made the lives of millions brighter. When he wrote *Make Your Life Worth While* and *Power Through Constructive Thinking* he left us clear and simple guide posts for Christian living.

"In recent years it seems fitting that Dr. Fox should take his work to Carnegie Hall, which had known the finest music. He brought to its time-honored halls the finest of thinking and Christly teaching. His rich humor and humble British dignity endeared him to thousands. His footprints are clearly established on the sands of time.

"The metaphysical movement claims Emmet Fox as one of its greatest leaders. Although he was ordained to the Christ Ministry by the Reverend Nona L. Brooks, co-founder of the Divine Science College in Denver, Colorado, and affiliated his New York work with this organization, his ministry reflected his own marked individuality. With the authority that arises out of a deep spiritual understanding and conviction, he spoke the Word of God with clear certainty and unwavering faith. The greatest monuments left to honor him are the mended lives of men and women everywhere who have found peace of mind, health of body and purposeful living through his teaching.

"Our hearts are deeply moved over the golden bowl that is broken, but our loving thoughts embrace the emerged Spirit that moves through timeless space in the Eternal Heart of God. Our gratitude and blessings reach out to our honored friend whom the hand of the Infinite Shepherd has anointed. In reverent faith we know that beyond the dim horizon of our vision his unseen lips still speak the words of God to a vaster congregation."